David L. Scott earned his Ph.D. in economics at the University of Arkansas and is a finance professor at Valdosta State College in Georgia. He has previously written seven books in such diverse areas as electric utilities, security investments, environmental pollution, managerial finance, and traveling in the national parks.

PRENTICE-HALL INTERNATIONAL, INC., *London*
PRENTICE-HALL OF AUSTRALIA PTY. LIMITED, *Sydney*
PRENTICE-HALL OF CANADA, LTD., *Toronto*
PRENTICE-HALL OF INDIA PRIVATE LIMITED, *New Delhi*
PRENTICE-HALL OF JAPAN, INC., *Tokyo*
PRENTICE-HALL OF SOUTHEAST ASIA PTE. LTD., *Singapore*
WHITEHALL BOOKS LIMITED, *Wellington, New Zealand*

david l. scott

STRETCHING YOUR INCOME

101 Ways to Help Beat Inflation

A SPECTRUM BOOK

Prentice-Hall, Inc., Englewood Cliffs, New Jersey 07632

Library of Congress Cataloging in Publication Data

SCOTT, DAVID LOGAN, (date)
  Stretching your income.

  "A Spectrum Book."
  Includes index.
  1. Finance, Personal. 2. Consumer education. I. Title
HG179.S345   332.024'02   81-15901
                            AACR2

ISBN 0-13-852723-7

ISBN 0-13-852715-6 {PBK.}

To Kay, who knows I practice what I preach

10   9   8   7   6   5   4   3   2   1

Editorial/production supervision by Carol Smith
Manufacturing buyer: Cathie Lenard

This Spectrum Book is available to businesses and organizations
at a special discount when ordered in large quantities.
For more information, contact Prentice-Hall, Inc., General Publishing Division,
Special Sales, Englewood Cliffs, N. J. 07632.

Contents

v

Preface

Double-digit inflation, wildly fluctuating interest rates, out-of-control government spending, high unemployment, skyrocketing energy bills . . . the list goes on and the implication is clear: as a consumer you probably need help in today's unpredictable economy. This book is dedicated to furnishing that help by providing money-saving ideas.

Here you will find 101 practical ways to fight inflation. The ideas are easy to implement and will help stretch your income just a little bit farther. You will discover how you can put each of the ideas to use and, in some cases, where you might go for additional help.

The content of this book spans the whole consumer spectrum: from financial topics concerning estate planning, budgeting, checking accounts, mutual funds, insurance, grocery shopping, and credit cards; to information on firewood, tires, milk, and memorial societies. Do you want to know about buying your own telephone? How about what kind of insurance to buy? Perhaps you have been considering insulating your water heater or buying a new car. You can even find out how to decide whether to buy large, medium, or small eggs the next time you go grocery shopping.

Though the subjects are diverse, they have a common thread: if put to use, each can save you money. Some of the topics involve a one-time effort to produce savings over a long period of time. You will find energy-saving ideas that could cut your costs year after year following only a small initial expenditure. Other ideas involve no additional expenditures, but merely suggest changes in the way you think about certain spending decisions. Some of the ideas you may already use. Others you may have considered but never put into practice because you were unsure if they actually worked. Hopefully, you will also run across a number of ideas that have never entered your mind. If you put only a few of the suggestions to work you should save many times the cost of this book. What a bargain!

David L. Scott
Valdosta, Georgia

chapter one

Preparing for the stretch

1. Think in Terms of What You Must Give Up
in Order to Buy Something

Economists often discuss an important idea they call *opportunity cost*. This refers to the cost of something in terms of its next best alternative. Suppose you have free tickets to the circus and are trying to decide whether to go or stay at home and watch a football game on television. If you go to the circus, the cost will be missing the game (and saving some transportation expenses). Alternatively, if you decide to watch the game, it will be at the cost of missing the circus.

The concept of opportunity cost also applies to personal financial management. One of the greatest mistakes many individuals make is to spend money on a good or service without stopping to think of what else could be purchased with the same funds. Many consumers decide they want something and simply buy it, even if they have to go into debt to do so. They do not stop and realize that using credit implies that they must eventually either give up the purchase of something else or be willing to work some additional hours. If you decide to trade an old car and $8,000 for a new sports car, then there is either $8,000 in other things you must forego or a great many additional hours you must be willing to work in order to earn that much money. In this case, if you are able to earn $4 per hour after taxes, you must work an additional 40 hours per week for an entire year. Before you sign on the dotted line ask yourself if what you are buying is worth what you are giving up. The same reasoning applies to less expensive purchases. If you decide to eat at a restaurant and spend $12 when you could eat at home for $4, the $8 difference must come from somewhere—perhaps it means missing a movie you would like to see or equals half the cost of a new toaster you have plans to purchase.

Constructing a personal budget, including the setting of financial goals, is one sure way of coming to grips with opportunity cost. Determining how much must periodically be set aside to purchase a new car, take a long vacation, or retire early illustrates the costs of attaining the goals and requires that you think in terms of what must be foregone—be it leisure time you must devote to earning additional income or other goods and services you would like to acquire. The next time you consider spending money, ask yourself how long you have to work to earn that much and what you may have to give up if you make the purchase. Evaluate the opportunity cost of your purchase.

2. Disregard Most Advertising

Every year American business pours tens of billions of dollars into various types of advertising promoting particular products in an effort to persuade you to make a purchase. Consumers are sometimes made aware of new products through advertisements, and many newspaper ads provide valuable price information. In addition, advertisements often provide information on where to buy particular products. Unfortunately, only a relatively small portion of advertising dollars is spent in a way that conveys any useful information to consumers. For example, in a single year, one of the country's largest consumer goods companies spent nearly a half-billion dollars in advertising on television alone. In spite of these huge expenditures, how much additional information that is really useful do you feel you have gained in the last year about toothpastes, laundry detergents, deodorants, hand soaps, coffees, soft drinks, paper towels, fast-food restaurants, and breakfast cereals?

Companies certainly do not spend all this money without the expectation that it will pay dividends in increased sales and profits. Much

of the advertising is directed toward convincing consumers that one product is significantly different from those of its competitors when, in fact,
the differences are actually quite small or nonexistent. This type of
advertising is especially prevalent in industries in which there are a few
large competitors. It is doubtful that consumers receive much benefit from
this advertising and, in fact, the end result may well be that prices to
consumers are higher because of it. The ultimate example of advertising
effectiveness is a producer being able to sell what is essentially the same
product under two different names at significantly different prices.

Unless a product's advertising conveys some useful information, such
as content or price, you should generally try to disregard it in making a
purchase decision. Let others pay the high prices that support the cost of
this advertising while you stick to making decisions on the basis of price
and quality.

3. Learn Some Basic Marketing Tricks

In an effort to convince consumers to purchase things they do not need,
buy products they do not know they need, or buy more than they ever
thought they would need, marketing people have developed a large
arsenal of weapons—some legal, some questionable, and others plainly
illegal. To compete against these sellers, you must understand the tactics
that are being used. In this way it is possible to avoid deals that may at
first seem good but are not. Or, even better, it may be possible to turn the
ruse around to your own benefit. Some of the more popular sales tactics
include:

Psychological Pricing.   Businesses often price their merchandise in
odd numbers such as 99 cents, or 88 cents because consumers tend to
think of these items in terms of 90 cents or 80 cents. (How many items
have you seen marked with prices ending in 81 cents or 91 cents?) A
$4.99 price appears to be much lower than a $5.00 price even though it
is not. If you watch for this tactic while shopping, you will be able to
avoid its influence.

Multiple Pricing.   Retailers have found that when they price an
item that usually sells for 20 cents at five for $1.00, they are able to
move more merchandise. Where consumers would normally purchase one

or two units, they may be influenced to buy five units under the multiple price. Be aware that it is not necessary to buy five units of a product marked five for $1.00 and you should be charged 20 cents for each unit you do purchase.

Combination Pricing.   Merchants will often offer a price on a group of products if a consumer purchases them all. This practice is most common in a restaurant where a combination price is offered for a sandwich, fries, and a drink. You may well find that the combination price is merely the sum of the individual prices and offers no savings. Even if there is some reduction in price, you may be required to buy something that would ordinarily be passed up. Compare the sum of prices on each of the individual items with the combination price before making a purchase.

Bait and Switch.   Businesses will sometimes offer a specially priced product in an advertisement. When a consumer attempts to buy the product, however, she will be told that the product is sold out, cannot be found, or is of inferior quality. Then the pitch is to convince the consumer to buy a higher-priced product that is available. Sellers of durable goods (appliances, tires, cars, furniture) are famous for this illegal tactic. In such a situation you should stick to your guns and demand to see the advertised merchandise.

Loss-Leader Pricing.   Stores will sometimes offer products at prices so low that they make little or no profit on their sales. The idea, of course, is to generate traffic and try to sell consumers other products at the same time. The idea for consumers is to grab up big quantities of the items that are being used as "loss leaders." Do not make the mistake of buying quantities so large that spoilage will result or buying even small quantities of items you will never use.

4. Subscribe to a Newspaper

The best shopping guide around can still be picked up at your very doorstep. That's right—the local newspaper about which your neighbors complain and whose price has been climbing higher and higher is probably still one of the best buys around. The reason is that a newspaper is as valuable for the information it provides to shoppers as it is for the news it supplies. In fact, the advertisements contained in newspapers are probably more useful to consumers than advertisements in any other medium because a higher proportion of newspaper ads are concerned with product availability and prices. Grocery stores advertise almost exclusively in newspapers. Retail chains (Sears, Penney, Montgomery Ward) and discounters (K Mart, Woolco) publicize their sales through newspapers. Restaurants advertise specials in local newspapers. And for some consumers, newspapers are the main source of cents-off coupons.

One of the most valuable sections of any newspaper is the classified advertisements. Here a careful reader may discover a variety of good buys in items ranging from $100,000 houses to used appliances. The advantages of buying directly from another individual is that you may be able to avoid helping to pay for a retailer's overhead (i.e., rent, utilities, and wages).

Of course, you can frequent a library and save the cost of a newspaper subscription. Or if you are only interested in grocery store ads and cents-off coupons, you can pick up individual copies of papers from a rack or newsstand (usually Wednesday evening or Thursday morning). The problem with these options is that you may well miss a single sale which would save the cost of a one- or two-month subscription to the paper.

As a general rule, it is best to subscribe to the local paper, even if it doesn't contain much news. If you want news, buy a big-city paper. What we are concerned with here is money-saving information to help you in making purchasing decisions.

One of the most valuable aspects of conscientiously reading through newspaper advertisements is that it gets you in tune with the local shopping scene. You begin to know which stores have the lowest prices, which offer the best sales, and, best of all, you begin to recognize a good buy when you see one. In addition, a newspaper allows you to make shopping decisions at home before you have to defend yourself against the marketing skills found in the stores.

5. Subscribe to <u>Consumer Reports</u>

Most goods and services are marketed with vague promises that they will make you more attractive to the opposite sex, are manufactured with old-fashioned pride, or are more refreshing than anything else available. It seems that advertisements contain very little information that is actually useful to consumers in allowing them to make rational choices among products. For example, how much hot water does a particular dishwasher model use? How nutritious is a meal at Burger King? How do the various brands of dishwashing liquid compare with respect to cleaning power? Over a period of time it is possible for a consumer to come to some general comparisons among competing products on the basis of trial and error. However, this is a relatively inaccurate, time-consuming, and expensive method of obtaining useful information.

A better method of improving your knowledge of product information is to religiously read *Consumer Reports*. This monthly publication of Consumers Union, a nonprofit corporation, contains a wealth of information that is valuable to consumers. Each issue includes a number of produce reports providing data that consumers should have prior to shopping. Products used for testing are purchased from stores (i.e., manufacturers are not allowed to submit models for testing) and the magazine typically ranks brands in the order of their estimated overall quality. The strong and weak points of each brand are generally noted. In addition to product tests and recommendations, the magazine also contains general articles on consumer topics such as no-fault insurance, automobile safety, diets, and government regulations. The annual December issue is a large *Buying Guide* which summarizes the results of tests conducted over a period of years. It also contains charts outlining frequency-of-repair records on a wide variety of automobile models. In order to keep its recommendations from being compromised, *Consumer Reports* contains no advertising and relies on subscription revenues to cover its expenses.

There is probably no better source of consumer information available than *Consumer Reports*. The annual subscription cost of $12 (*Consumer Reports*, P.O. Box 1941, Marion, Ohio 43305) can easily be recovered in a single purchase. For those of you who do not want to shell out the $12 or who want to sample a few issues first, try the public library. Nearly every library is a subscriber. The main advantage of subscribing is that you can save old issues for reference. You might consider sharing the magazine and its subscription cost with a friend.

6. Buy Extra Copies of Newspapers That Contain Coupons You Can Use

Many newspaper and magazine readers are at least occasional coupon clippers. A 50-cents-off coffee coupon here and a 10-cents-off coupon on cheese slices there. Smokers are able to take advantage of numerous coupons for dollar reductions on cigarette cartons or even free packs of cigarettes. Unless you are really into couponing you may run across no more than one or two coupons that interest you in a newspaper's weekly food section (usually the Wednesday evening or Thursday morning edition). In some cases you may see coupons for merchandise you buy, but the amount of savings is so small that it is not worth 7 cents to clip the coupon and remember to carry it to the store.

In spite of some newspapers offering little or no worthwhile coupons, a reader will occasionally run across issues that prove to be coupon bonanzas. Some manufacturers may use coupons for unusually large discounts, or even free merchandise, as methods of enticing consumers to try new or "improved" products. In the last few years, manufacturers have provided coupons for free cigarettes, liquid sugar, cake mix, imitation cheese slices, and candy bars. Others provide cents-off coupons for products you use. In either instance potential savings may equal several dollars on the coupons contained in a single paper.

Most manufacturers that use coupons provide a restriction that a consumer not use more than one coupon per item purchased. In other words, you are not allowed to use four 10-cents-off coupons on a single can of tomato soup. However, no such limitation is generally applicable to using the four coupons on the purchase of four cans of tomato soup. As a result, if a paper contains a number of different coupons for products you use or if it has an especially valuable coupon or two, it may be worth the expense to purchase a half-dozen or more copies of that paper if the coupons far more than offset the cost of the additional papers.

A key to engaging in this type of operation is to examine the paper early enough so that you will be able to purchase additional copies. Also observe the coupons' expiration dates and consider how frequently you use particular products so that you do not overbuy and have merchandise spoil. Beware the temptation to purchase items you would not ordinarily use just because a coupon is available.

7. Try for a Refunding "Triple Play"

Companies use cents-off coupons in order to entice consumers to use their products. The coupons may be occasioned by intense competition among companies, the introduction of a new product, or as a temporary incentive to overcome consumer resistance to a recent price increase. Cents-off coupons are not cheap for companies to use since they pay to get the coupons distributed (usually by means of newspapers and magazines) and must pay a service fee (usually 5¢ or 7¢ per coupon) to the stores that accept them. This is in addition to reimbursing the stores for the face amount of the coupons. Recent revelations that many coupons are being fraudulently redeemed without purchase of the required merchandise means that there is yet an added cost to this marketing tool.

Since promoting merchandise with coupons can be a relatively expensive process and, in any case, is successful with only a part of the population, companies also try other methods of convincing consumers to try a product. For example, they sometimes offer savings off the regular price through cents-off specials printed on the box, jar, or can. Or they may offer retailers special buys so that stores can run the products as featured items at reduced prices. In addition, companies often allow consumers to send in code numbers, labels, or portions of packages for refunds.

One way to achieve extra savings is to combine coupons, store specials, and refunds (hence the heading's "triple play"). However, since companies often try these various marketing techniques at different times, you must be patient and observant. When you clip coupons, observe the expiration dates and then hold them until some other form of savings is available to you. The most valuable coupons are the ones with no expiration dates, for these can be held indefinitely. Unfortunately, except for a few firms like Procter & Gamble (Gleem, Crest, Crisco, Ivory, Pringle's, Coast, etc.), companies rarely issue coupons without expiration dates.

Although this procedure may sound like more trouble than it is worth, you will be surprised how many times it is possible to combine coupons with the additional savings of sales or refunds. You can sometimes actually reduce a product's cost to near zero if you really hit it right. In order to be successful at this game, you must keep track of your coupons and their expiration dates. In addition, you must be a regular reader of newspaper advertisements in order to spot the specials where your coupons can be used.

chapter two

General tips for stretching your income

8. Avoid Impulse Buying

Successful business executives carefully plan their firm's purchases. They decide upon the goods and services that are required to carry on operations and then seek to secure the best possible prices. Successful consumers operate in the same manner. Most of all, they suppress a natural human inclination to buy impulsively. When consumers buy things without using proper forethought they tend to pay too much or to purchase goods and services they do not need. Businesses operated in such a manner are not long for this world. Consumers that consistently buy on impulse may remain in operation but do so in a state of financial difficulty.

If successful businessmen do not buy impulsively themselves, they often try to take advantage of consumers' tendency to do so. Retail stores are frequently laid out in a manner that stimulates impulse buying. For example, most retail stores have special displays to increase sales of particular products. Supermarkets and discount stores place impulse items such as chewing gum, cigarettes, candy bars, and magazines next to checkout lanes in the hope that you will pick a few up and throw them on the counter with your other purchases. Department stores locate merchandise displays just inside their front doors or at the bottom of down escalators, knowing that they will catch your eye. Supermarkets put large pyramids of cans in the middle of the aisle so that you nearly run into them. Clothing store managers, knowing that shoppers buy impulsively, place tables or racks of dresses, ties, shirts, pants, and coats in strategic locations. Meanwhile, manufacturers spend big money in packaging their products to stimulate impulse buying.

As a general rule, items that are displayed in such a manner as to stimulate impulse buying either have high profit margins or are products that stores are particularly eager to get rid of. This does not mean they are necessarily bad buys, since a retailer may be closing out an item by offering an especially good price. However, you should be sure that the merchandise is something you really need and that it is not out of date.

There are a couple of methods you can use to fight impulse buying. First, before you pick up a product from a special display, stop and ask yourself why the retailer has the product there in the first place. However, the best way to curb a tendency to buy impulsively is to make out a shopping list and stick to buying the items on the list. When you go into a store know exactly what it is you are supposed to buy there and avoid everything else. Just remember when you see those special displays and fancy wrappings that the manufacturer and retailer are in cahoots trying to take advantage of your weakness. Show them both that you are too strong for their tricks by passing right on by.

9. Do Not Buy When a Salesperson Puts on Too Much Pressure

Have you ever been talked into buying something and then later wondered how it could have happened? Well, do not feel all alone since the same thing has happened to the best of us. One of the best ways to keep this from recurring is to allow yourself time to consider a purchase before actually making it. People are most likely to make a decision they will regret when they do not take or are not allowed to take the time to consider the pros and cons of making a particular purchase. This does not mean you should spend a half-hour pondering what size toothpaste to buy or deciding whether to buy lettuce today. It does mean, however, that you should carefully consider major purchases.

One of the primary reasons people make purchases they later regret is that salespeople convince them to do so. High-pressure sales tactics are many times based on the presumption that if you are given enough time to think about a purchase, you will probably decline to make it. Thus, they try to convince you to sign an agreement or actually pay for a product before you get away. Such tactics should be a clear warning that the product or service under consideration may well be of questionable value.

Some groups are infamous for using high-pressure approaches on consumers. A number of land development companies raised the practice to an art form during the 1960s and 1970s before the government cracked down on them. Many car salesmen have closed deals with shaky prospects by utilizing the hard sell. And door-to-door salespeople hawking everything from encyclopedia sets to magazine subscriptions to pots and pans generally base their entire presentation on the proposition that they must convince you to buy before they leave.

Any time a salesperson puts on too much pressure, you should probably avoid buying the product. At least give yourself time to carefully consider the purchase. If they are that anxious to get you to buy whatever it is they are selling, they will almost surely still be willing to sell it at a later date. And if you are told that there are only a few left, take your chances. If the deal is that good and there are so few units left to sell, there should be no reason to give you the hard sell. And if the pressure comes from a door-to-door salesperson, a general rule is to pass up the purchase, whatever it happens to be, even if you are told you can later change your mind.

There are some remedies available to consumers who buy things under pressure. One section of the U.S. Uniform Commercial Code states that courts may void unconscionable contracts. Although whether a particular contract is unconscionable or not is a subjective judgment, one drawn up through high-pressure sales tactics might qualify. The problem is that a consumer must generally sue in order to recover. Consumers have more hope in voiding a purchase from a door-to-door salesperson. Here you are given the right to cancel within three days any purchase of $25 or more. The salesperson is required to inform you of the cancellation right and provide two copies of the proper form. For more information write Federal Trade Commission, 6th Floor, Gelman Building, 2120 L Street N.W., Washington, D.C. 20037.

While there are consumer laws that apply to these situations, what the law says and what actually happens may be two different things. The best policy is to take your time in the first place rather than trying to right a wrong at a later time.

10. Buy Basic Models

So you just bought a new car with power seats, power windows, a power antenna, cruise control, a station-seeking quadraphonic radio, and a motorized trunk-release mechanism. You say your washing machine has so many controls that it took almost two months to learn how to use it correctly. Maybe you are most proud of that new dishwasher with such a wide variety of cycles that it cleans anything from paper plates to the charcoal grill.

A common mistake of many individuals when buying cars, appliances, or other merchandise is to include an excessive number of gadgets and frills. From an economic standpoint this is generally not a wise move. A better course of action is to buy the most basic model of an item that is available.

Basic models of almost anything have a lower initial price. Since it costs the manufacturer more to add gadgets and frills to a product, a higher price will be charged in the marketplace for the finished good or service. You do not get a power antenna for free. In addition to the higher production costs, manufacturers and retailers frequently place higher markups on models with extra gadgets such as those that are top-of-the-line. Over the years, it has not been unusual for the automobile companies to place higher markups on options than on the cars themselves. Thus, a car radio that retails for $120 may cost the manufacturer $60—a 100% increase—while the basic automobile only carries a 30% markup. Another reason basic models often cost less to buy is because more price competition exists at that end of the product line. As an example, basic color television sets are often sold at extremely competitive prices (i.e., a very small profit) in order to draw customer traffic. Once the customer hits the store he may make some other purchases and a salesperson can always show him a more expensive model.

You must also consider how much of the additional cost you will recover if you plan to eventually sell the product. How much extra will you recover if your car has a vinyl top and power windows, for example? Or, when you trade in your washing machine how many more dollars will you receive because it has a selection of cycles? You probably know the answer. Frills and gadgets do not bring much from people that shop for used merchandise.

Perhaps most important, products with a lot of gadgets tend to break down more often. The more controls something has and the more complicated it is, the more often you must have it repaired and the more it will cost to repair. So the fancy model not only costs more to buy, it also costs more to keep. Do yourself a favor and stay with the basics.

11. Buy Ahead

Do you remember the last time you ran out of mustard and had to run to the small convenience store down the street? Or the time you ran low on toilet paper or facial tissue and could not find it on sale anywhere? And how about when you had to buy laundry detergent because you ran out? Each of these instances probably resulted in your paying a higher price than you otherwise would have because you were in a hurry to buy.

One of the best methods of saving money on the products you need is to plan and buy ahead. This allows you, rather than the stores, to be in the driver's seat. If you start shopping for products before you actually require them, it is more likely you can buy exactly what you want and do it at the right price because you have time to watch for sales, coupons, and refunds. It is when you do not plan ahead and have to purchase items on short notice that you really get stuck.

Of course, not all products lend themselves to this type of shopping. For example, it would be difficult to buy large appliances such as refrigerators and ovens in this manner since they are so costly and can be difficult to store. Likewise, perishable items, such as fresh fruits and vegatables, cannot be purchased very far in advance. Many items are quite suitable for advance purchase, however. Health and beauty aids like soap, facial cream, shampoo, and razor blades should always be bought in advance. Likewise, paper products such as facial tissue, paper towels, and toilet paper and cleaning aids like dishwasher detergent, laundry detergent, and toilet bowl cleaner are things that you should always keep on hand. Many food items for the kitchen such as ketchup, mustard, spices, powdered milk, soup, peanut butter, salad dressings, sugar, and cooking oil can be purchased in sufficient quantities so that you never run out. Even some clothing like jogging shoes, socks, and undergarments should be bought and stored for the time they are eventually needed.

Granted, buying ahead does have a few disadvantages. First of all, these things will take up space in your house or apartment so that you are somewhat limited by the storage area you have available. Second, it can be argued that there is a cost to this madness since you are tying up money in these products that could be put in the bank to earn interest. This is a valid argument, of course, but it must be balanced against the fact that general price increases would cause the goods to cost more in the future. Thus, peanut butter which normally sells at $1.60, but is currently on sale for $1.20, may well cost $1.75 next year. The higher price you must pay if you delay your purchase will more than wipe out the extra income you would earn by investing the $1.20. Even if you are able to find the product on sale next year, there is every reason to expect that the future sale price will be higher than the current one.

12. Buy Generic or Store Brands

As you bend over to pick up a couple of cans of corn that sell for 42¢ each, you spot the nonbranded (*generic*) cans that are priced at three for a dollar. Later, when you reach the dairy case and start to grab the 49-cent yogurt, you notice that the supermarket also sells its own brand for 39 cents. Across the road at the discount store you find the national brand of paper towels selling for 69 cents while the store's brand costs only 59 cents. What is going on here? The house brand must be inferior to the national brand or it could not sell at a lower price? Or could it?

Many chains, including drugstores, supermarkets, discount stores, hardware stores, and general merchandise stores, are increasingly stocking their shelves with merchandise bearing either their own brand names or no brand name at all. As a rule, these products are less expensive than their national brand counterparts. However, the lower price does not necessarily infer that the quality is lower, and the products are sometimes identical to brands that carry a higher price.

Large retail chains usually do not own their own buildings nor manufacture their own merchandise. They prefer to have their money tied up in the products they carry than in real estate and factories. These firms contract with companies that manufacture or process a particular product. Although the house brand will be a direct competitor to the manufacturer's own product, the economics of bargaining on such a contract are compelling. First of all, if the manufacturer rejects the offer, the chain can turn to a competing supplier. Second, the manufacturer is often able to increase production at low cost because he is set up to produce at a higher volume than he is currently turning out. Third, a large chain has the potential to place huge orders, allowing lower quantity prices. For these reasons, chains are often able to bargain with manufacturers and processors for low prices. This allows them to charge consumers low prices for nonbranded or house brand products.

An equally important reason that generic and house brands usually cost less than national brands is because their prices do not have to be set to recover large advertising expenditures. These expenditures must be passed on to consumers in the prices of the products. A portion of the price you pay when buying a national brand is for image and not for the product's contents. You might look at the prices of generic or house brands as sort of bare bones.

This is not meant to imply that generic and house brands are always identical in quality to national brands. Some items may be of significantly lower quality so that you do not find them to be good buys even at the lower prices. If you do not believe this, just ask those individuals that have tried one-ply generic toilet paper. Many times the judgment between brands is subjective and varies from one consumer to another. The only way to make your own decision is to give the less-expensive generic and house brands a try. Some you will probably like and continue to use. At the very least, you may break the habit of assuming national brands are better just because they are more familiar.

13. Buy Multiple Units of Sale Items

As consumers become more price-conscious it is an increasingly common practice for them to pick up a few sale items while shopping. Many individuals will even buy an extra unit or two if a sale is particularly good. The real secret of saving money on a sale is not to buy two or three units, but ten, twelve, or even more units. In other words, you should really load up on products when the prices are especially favorable. Of course, to buy this much the product should be something you will use: it is a mistake to buy even a single unit of something you do not use. Also, the product must be something that can be stored if you plan to buy a dozen or more units.

Fortunately, stores are often accommodating in providing sales on things you can use and that are relatively easy to store. In particular, health and beauty aids such as toothpaste, soap, razor blades, shampoo, and hand lotions are regularly offered at reduced prices at discount, drug, and variety stores. Supermarkets often run specials on canned goods such as vegetables, tuna fish, and fruit juices. In addition, you can generally find paper towels, facial tissue, and toilet paper on sale somewhere. If you are a consistent reader of a newspaper or shopper you will be able to recognize a sale price that is unusually good from one that is only mediocre. It is the particularly good sale when you should really stock up. You may want to purchase at least enough units to last until the next big sale.

Stores will sometimes place a limit on the units of a sale item an individual is permitted to purchase. Some shoppers will attempt to bypass this restriction by using different checkout lanes, by visiting the store more than once during a sale period, or by making purchases at different stores if more than one location is available in the same town. You may find it useful to plan a trip to the store when your family is along (limits are nearly always on an individual rather than a family basis) or when you are with friends. In addition, if you ask the store manager, you may be permitted to purchase more than the stated limit (don't ask for an unreasonable number). Grocery stores often restrict sale items to shoppers that have some minimum purchase (say, $7.50 or $10.00). If you are with someone else and are planning to purchase a large amount of groceries, you might consider using two carts. Or, if you are alone, you might want to fill only part of your list and then return to finish shopping and check out through a different lane.

Even though most of the products discussed here have a relatively long life, they do not last forever. Thus, you should use some care in their storage. When you store the sale items in your home or apartment (you might consider the area under your beds if you are really short on space), be sure to place the new merchandise behind that which you already have so that you will use the old items first.

14. Buy Durable Goods When They Are out of Season

If you are the kind of person who waits until the last minute to buy something, then you are probably paying top dollar. The reason is that the very time you need things most is often when they are also in the greatest demand by others who are acting in the same manner as you. Thus, you buy the artificial Christmas tree the second week in December, a wool sweater in September, an electric blanket during the first cold snap, and the new air conditioner on the first day the temperature hits 95 degrees.

One way to save money on durable goods is to buy them out of season. This does not apply to food, of course, since food items are not considered durable goods. What we are talking about here are goods that last for a relatively long time so that you have control over the timing of a purchase. Things like clothing and appliances are durable goods. Not all durable goods are seasonal, of course, so that it is not always possible to buy something when nobody else wants it. Television sets exhibit relatively steady sales on a year-round basis, for instance.

Retailers normally build up inventories in anticipation of expected sales. Since seasonal items sell mainly during certain weeks or months of each year, this type of merchandise will be heavily stocked on the weeks during and immediately preceding the time of greatest demand. A retailer may order more than he or she expects to sell to keep from running short when sales are at a peak. Shortages not only result in lost sales, they also lose customers. Once a selling period has passed, the retailer must generally keep the merchandise until the next year, or send it back to the manufacturer (if this is permitted), or sell the items at big markdowns to keep from using the first two options. This is the time for you to jump in.

What types of goods should you be looking for? How about lawn mowers in the late summer or fall? Or winter clothes in February or March? Try buying air conditioners in October or November when nobody else wants them. Some of the best buys occur in holiday-related items since the wait until the next selling season is so long and because the season when the products are in demand is so short that very large overstocks can occur. Thus, if you wait until the day after Christmas, an artificial Christmas tree can frequently be purchased for half the price that was asked only a few days earlier. The same applies to cards and ornaments that the retailer would have to store for another year. You should keep in mind that many merchants are more agreeable to price bargaining on merchandise that has just passed its peak selling period. If you see some out-of-season merchandise in a store, try a little negotiating with the manager.

A policy of purchasing durable goods when they are out of season will require planning and self-discipline on your part. You must have funds available to make the purchases and you cannot miss an opportunity because you know it is possible to wait until later. The later time will most likely be when the goods are again in season and selling for their regular prices.

15. Ask for a Rain Check

Although stores are supposed to have adequate supplies of advertised specials, for one reason or another they will often run out. Perhaps the manager underestimated how much consumers would want. Maybe a transportation mixup has delayed arrival of a shipment. Possibly the store stocked only a minimal amount of the product because the manager did not want to sell many units at the advertised price.

 If you go to a store and find the shelf space for an advertised special is bare, you should not just mumble to yourself and leave. First tell a clerk that the shelf is empty and ask if any more of the product is available. You will frequently find that the shelf is only temporarily empty because the employees have not noticed or have not had time to restock it. You may also find that special displays of the product are in a different area of the store. If the clerk informs you that the store is out of the product and no additional shipments will be arriving prior to the end of the sale, you should immediately ask for a rain check. You may have to see the cashier or go to the office, but most businesses will provide you with a rain check if you will only ask. As all good shoppers know, a rain check is a slip of paper that permits you to purchase a product at its sale price after the sale has ended. You must be careful, however, for many rain checks will have their own expiration dates—often two to three weeks after they are issued. Do not feel that you are inconveniencing the store by asking for a rain check. After all, you have made a special trip to buy a product that the store is advertising and it is not your fault that none is available. If anyone should be upset, it is you.

 Rain checks might well provide you with some advantages that are not available if the product is in stock. Stores will often place a limit on the number of units of the sale item you are allowed to buy, but this limit will many times be left off the rain check when it is written. Thus, you may have a chance to "stock up" when the product comes in. Another advantage of rain checks is that they give you extra time to look for cents-off coupons on the product. Manufacturers often promote their products by first offering retailers special buys so that they will, in turn, run their own specials (hence the sale). Once this type of promotion is over, the manufacturer may follow up with cents-off coupons to keep consumers coming back for more. If you have a rain check, you may be able to use the coupons against the sale price rather than the regular price.

16. Observe the Amounts That Clerks Ring Up

If you were required to stand behind a cash register for hours at a time and ring up hundreds or thousands of items speeding beside you on an endless black belt, can you imagine not making a mistake every so often? Of course not. And if the prices of the items were constantly changing, the chance of making a mistake would be multiplied. There is no reason to suspect that the vast majority of clerks intentionally try to cheat consumers by overcharging them. It is just that with the multitude of transactions they must record, it is not possible to be perfect.

There are a couple of ways to try to guard against being overcharged. Some individuals keep their register tapes and check off the items and prices when the goods are unsacked at home. Although this may be better than no checking at all, it presents a number of difficulties. First, it can be quite time-consuming. If you purchase much merchandise, it will be necessary to return to the store in order to voice your complaint. Unless you repack all of the merchandise and take it back with you, there is no way for the clerk or manager to know if you are telling the truth or trying to pull a fast one.

A second approach to keep from being overcharged is to observe the amounts that clerks ring up on the cash register. The key to doing this is to get organized and be ready when your turn at the register comes. Don't be putting items on the counter, digging in your pockets for money, searching for coupons, starting to write a check, or—worst of all—reading a magazine when the clerk begins processing your order. Have as much of this done as possible before the clerk starts. If you do not have time to place all your merchandise on the counter before the clerk finishes with the person in front of you, simply mention that you would like for him or her to wait a few seconds until you are ready.

Inaccurate ring-ups can be expected to occur most frequently when a store is quite busy and there is a big line behind you. The clerk will be in a rush and is more likely to make a mistake. Mistakes, especially overrings, are also more likely to occur in stores that do not reprice the items that are on sale. Many stores will run daily or weekly specials on selected merchandise and, rather than going to the expense of retagging every item that is on sale (and then retagging it again when the sale is over), will rely on the clerks to remember the specials at the checkout line. There is no way that every clerk will remember every item on sale. As a result, unless you are careful, it is inevitable that you will occasionally be charged the regular price on a sale item. The moral to this story is to be an alert consumer. Be ready when your bill is being rung up and keep a list of the specials and their respective prices at hand.

Watching the register is less important when computerized checking with a scanner is used. Sale prices are programmed into the computer so that mistakes like the ones mentioned here should not occur. One of the major advantages for a store using this type of system is that it is not necessary to reprice all the merchandise every time a price change occurs. Until such a system becomes more widespread, it is to your advantage to remain alert in the checkout line.

17. Try to Pay Some Bills in Cash

You have probably forgotten that it is still possible to pay bills in cash. Most people have become so used to making payments by means of checks and credit cards that they have forgotten businesses will still accept good old cash. Of course, you must be ready to accept the strange looks that come your way when you count out those tens and fives. But just think, you will not have to produce any identification, and the clerk will not have to call a toll-free-number to find out if your money is still in good standing.

So you can save time and trouble by paying in cash. How can you save money, you ask? If you normally pay all of your bills by mail with checks, you can save money in two ways. The monthly cost of stamps and envelopes can add up to more than you think. Suppose you normally pay eight or ten monthly bills such as those for your telephone, electricity, gas, water and sewer, and mortgage or rent by mail. With the cost of first-class postage soon going to 20 or 25 cents, it is possible to save $2.00 to $2.50 per month ($30.00 annually) by merely skipping the post office. A second savings results for those people who generally keep such a small balance in their checking account that they are charged for each check they write. With a normal fee of 10 cents per check plus an average cost of 2½ cents each to buy the checks (a box of 200 checks usually costs about

$5), paying in cash will save an additional 12 cents each time real money is substituted for a check. Thus, this should save you another $12 to $15 annually.

If you are a person who inadvertently writes overdrafts, you will quite likely be doing yourself a favor by reducing the number of checks you write because it will also reduce the possibility of losing track of your checking account balance. And if you normally pay by credit card, your use of cash will help the merchants since they will save the portion of your payment that they are normally required to forward to the credit card issuer.

Do not carry this suggestion to extremes. It is not possible to save money by driving 5 miles out of your way in order to keep from using a 20-cent stamp. However, in many instances it is possible to take care of bills while you are on your normal shopping route. This is especially true for utility bills which can often be paid at selected banks and stores as well as at the utility's main office. Plus, there just seems to be something rewarding about paying a bill with real money. Be sure to ask for a receipt.

18. Purchase the Lowest-Cost Alternative
Unless There Is a Good Reason to Do Otherwise

Maybe you have heard the old saying "You get what you pay for." Sometimes you pay more and do receive a significantly better product. At other times you pay more and get robbed. And even if a higher-priced item is better, it may not be enough better to justify the cost difference.

Businesses consider many factors in pricing their products. Some of these factors, such as the cost of materials and labor, may be directly related to product quality. Higher prices may also indicate inefficient production, low and costly output levels, high promotion and distribution expenses, or high manufacturer and retailer markups. In other words, some of the major costs of production often have little relation to product quality. For example, many businesses have high advertising budgets to convince consumers of their products' superiority. This results in inflated costs of products to cover advertising expenses in addition to direct production costs. Using this method, companies are able to turn out identical products with different names and sell them at significantly different prices. This applies to products such as clothing, foods, and appliances.

A business may decide to set a price above that of the competition in order to give consumers the impression that the quality of the product is superior. They know many people believe "you get what you pay for," so if something costs more, they will assume it must be better. As a bonus to the seller, some consumers buy higher-priced items simply for status—to show they can afford them. For years Americans willingly paid significantly higher prices for certain automobile models even though their manufacturing costs were not much more than some models with much lower pricetags. Was this a case of car buyers getting what they were paying for? Hardly. At least not in the form of product quality. It was more a case of paying for an image.

How does a smart consumer break out of this trap of buying over-priced products? In the case of less expensive merchandise such as food items and personal care products, you should be willing to experiment. Try some other, lower-price brands and see how they compare to the product you normally buy. You may be surprised to find that a less expensive soap is every bit as good as the one you have used for the last ten years. And you could discover a lesser-known make of canned peas that your family cannot tell from the more expensive variety you have been serving. With higher-priced merchandise such as appliances and automobiles it is not practical to engage in trial-and-error buying. Before purchasing one of these items you should research some consumer magazines and talk to friends. Use someone else's experience to compare quality and price. And remember that unless there is evidence to the contrary, you should operate on the assumption that the lowest-cost alternative offers the better value.

chapter three

Stretching financial resources

19. Start a Personal Budget

Do you find it difficult to make ends meet from one payday to the next? Maybe you need to start a personal budget. A budget is not a cure-all to your financial problems and it surely will not create additional money out of thin air. It will, however, allow you to know where you are, make you decide where you are going, and indicate how you will get there. Most important of all, a budget will force you to make some hard choices by showing you in black and white what is financially possible and what is not.

How do you start a budget? First, construct a balance sheet by taking an inventory to determine where you are. This involves listing what you own (your assets) and what you owe (your liabilities), including the current monetary value of each. The end result of this is to subtract the total of the liabilities from the total assets in order to find your net worth. If you cashed in just enough assets to pay off all your debts this is what you would have left.

The next step is to determine your goals—for example, paying for your children to go to college, owning your house free and clear in twenty

years, taking a trip to Europe in five years, and building a certain retirement fund by the time you are sixty-five. Even smaller things such as
purchasing a car and buying new appliances should be included. It is possible to incorporate these infrequently purchased items into the budgeting
process by deciding how much must be set aside each period in order to
achieve these goals.

In establishing a budget it is necessary to estimate your income and
expenditures over a time period. This may be done on a monthly, weekly,
or biweekly basis, depending upon which is most convenient and how
often you are paid. With practice you will be able to do this for a year.
Although income may be relatively easy to determine, you will probably
have some initial trouble estimating expenditures. This is to be expected
as most people begin the budgeting process on a trial-and-error basis. It is
important not to get bogged down in detail by recording very small expenditures (e.g., chewing gum). You might keep track of these payments
over a short period to get an idea of the cost and then include them in a
"miscellaneous" category. The key to successful budgeting is to keep at
it and to refine the spending estimates as you go. Even in the early stages
of constructing a budget when the spending estimates are not very accurate, the income estimates will allow you to determine the expenditures
that can be made over a given period without going into debt.

For an easily understandable booklet (14 pages) on this subject
call or visit your local U.S. Department of Agriculture county extension
agent and ask for Home and Garden Bulletin Number 108, *A Guide to
Budgeting for the Family* (it is free). You may also obtain a free copy by
writing to the U.S. Department of Agriculture, Office of Governmental
and Public Affairs, Washington, D.C. 20250 and asking for the booklet
by title. Another source of detailed information on constructing a budget
is your local library. Most books on personal finance or personal money
management include a chapter on budgeting. They nearly always include
sample forms that can be copied.

20. Establish an Emergency Fund

Every individual should have a fund of money that can be quickly tapped
in an emergency. Even though this type of fund provides a relatively low
return, the sacrifice of income is worthwhile. Not only will your peace of

mind benefit from having such a fund, but the practical aspects are simply overwhelming.

Many of the money-saving suggestions in this book are based on the presumption that a person has an emergency fund available. These suggestions include not carrying collision and comprehensive insurance on an old car, using deductibles when you insure things, accepting a long waiting period when buying a disability-income policy, and not buying service contracts on appliances. Every one of these recommendations requires that funds be available in case one or more of the losses are encountered. The reduction of income caused by funds being placed in a low-yielding emergency fund, rather than a long-term investment, should be more than offset by the savings that are made possible by implementing these other suggestions.

How much should a person set aside in an emergency fund? The answer depends upon the expenses the fund may be required to support. You need to coordinate the amount of funds you have available on short-term notice with the possible losses you may incur. Most financial advisors suggest that you have from three to six months of after-tax income available. However, this is just a suggestion since factors such as those mentioned above must also be considered. The more losses you may have to support by drawing on the fund, the larger the fund should be.

Where should a person establish such a fund? Initially, it is probably just as good to use some type of passbook account at a credit union, commercial bank, or savings and loan association. Your choice may be limited by what is available in your locality. Try to obtain as high a return as possible without sacrificing the ability to draw from the fund quickly and without penalty. Choose an institution that pays interest from the day of deposit to the day of withdrawal if you will be making frequent withdrawals and you do not have to sacrifice too much in the way of return. Once your fund has grown in size you might consider buying shares in a mutual fund that purchases investments normally available only to investors with large amounts of money. Withdrawals may be made with little trouble from these money-market mutual funds, and many will even allow investors to write checks on their balances. The advantage of using money-market funds is that the return is usually significantly higher than the return on savings accounts. Since a minimum initial investment of about $1,000 is generally required, it will be necessary to accumulate this amount before being able to use this as an emergency fund (thus the savings account). For further information on these funds talk to a broker-age company or look through an issue of the *Wall Street Journal* for these funds' advertisements.

21. Join a Credit Union

Credit unions are cooperative associations that are organized to promote thrift among their members. In simple terms, a credit union accumulates the savings of some members and uses these funds to make loans to other members. Although banks and savings and loan associations basically do about the same thing, credit unions are generally run in such a manner that the spread between the rates charged to borrowers and the rates paid to savers are narrower. In other words, it is quite likely you can get a better deal as either a saver or a borrower at a credit union than you can at most other financial institutions.

Credit unions are generally organized through a union, a business, or a fraternal organization, with membership restricted to employees or members (or their relatives) of the sponsoring organization. Once you join a credit union you will be able to remain a member even if you quit the sponsoring organization. While there may be no credit union which you are eligible to join, it is possible that there may actually be one but you do not know it. How easy is it to join a credit union if you are eligible? The entrance fee is usually quite nominal and you are generally required to buy one share (savings) at a cost of $5. The $5 is returned if you decide to quit.

This brings us back to the statement made above. Why is it that credit unions can typically operate much like commercial banks but at lower cost? There are actually a number of reasons. First, space for the credit union's operations may be donated by the business or union that sponsors it. Second, in many cases much of the necessary work is per-formed on a volunteer basis. In addition, since members may be well known to the credit union directors, it is less likely there will be unpaid loans.

A credit union is a particularly good place to keep savings in an easy-to-get emergency fund since it almost always pays a higher return than do banks and savings and loan associations on passbook accounts. Be sure to check that savings accounts at the credit union you choose are insured.

In addition, credit unions will usually offer loans on durable items like automobiles and appliances at lower rates than do other lenders. Early repayment of loans is generally not penalized, and credit life insurance to pay off the loan in case of a borrower's death is usually provided at no extra charge.

22. Keep the Required Minimum Balance in
Your Checking Account and Avoid a Monthly Service Charge

Most banks now determine your monthly checking account service charge on the basis of the number of checks you write per month plus a set fee. For example, a typical bank might set its monthly charge at $1.50 plus 10 cents for each check that clears the bank since the last statement. Thus, if you write 30 checks during a month (and these checks are presented to the bank for payment), your account will be charged with a $4.50 service fee.

Many banks that set their fees in this manner (and most do) also provide that if you keep your checking account balance from dropping below a certain level, there will be no charge levied against you for that particular month. The justification is that if a customer has a sufficient amount of funds in his or her account, the bank is able to earn enough money by loaning the funds out to offset the costs of administering the account. On the other hand, a person who consistently has a balance close to zero should be charged for the service the bank provides.

Suppose you are a customer of the above-mentioned bank and that it has a policy of not imposing a monthly fee if your account has not dropped below $300 at any time since your last statement was processed. Like most customers, you normally deposit your paycheck at the end of each pay period and then allow your balance to drop to near zero by the time you are paid again. Any excess funds are put into a savings account where they can earn interest. Thus, if you write an average of 30 checks per month, your annual charges will total about 12 X $4.50, or $54.00. Now suppose you decide to avoid the checking fee by disciplining yourself to always keeping a minimum of $300. Is this smart? Well, you are able to save $54 annually with a $300 investment, resulting in an annual return of $54/$300, or 18%. Not bad! And remember that this is the tax-free return since the checking account fee is not tax-deductible. Now compare this tax-free return with the return you can earn if you keep the $300 elsewhere. It is quite doubtful you can do better. Of course, your annual return from keeping the minimum balance depends upon the bank's fees and the number of checks you normally write. If you are unsure of the fee your bank charges, give it a call.

23. Think Twice Before Joining a Bank Club

Most banks offer a package of financial services under an impressive name such as the Gold Key Account or Executive Club Account. The customer pays $4 or $5 per month and generally receives free checking account service, free personalized checks, travelers checks with no service fee, a reduced rate of interest on personal loans, free or reduced rental on a safe-deposit box, and overdraft protection so money will be automatically transferred to the customer's checking account if a check is written for more than his or her balance. Some clubs also provide members with free travel insurance and reduced prices on group vacation trips.

Many people join a bank club for one reason—free checking. If this is the only reason, joining is almost surely a bad buy unless they write an unusually large number of checks. Whether joining one of these clubs is a good buy for you depends upon the services you use. Suppose you are really interested only in free checking, free checks, and a free safe-deposit box. You either already have the other services (for free) or are not interested in them. Depending upon where you live, small safe-deposit boxes usually rent for $10 to $15 per year. Let us assume you could rent one for $12. Let us also suppose you write about 200 checks annually which you are able to purchase for $4.50. The cost of your regular checking account will depend upon the bank's policy. If the standard charge is 10 cents per check plus $1.00 per month, then your annual cost should be in the vicinity of $32 (i.e., 200 X 10 cents plus 12 X $1.00). Thus, these three items are costing you $48.50 annually. If the bank club costs $4 per month ($48 annually) and you do not desire any additional services, the choice is a toss-up. Now suppose the bank has a policy of not charging for checking accounts so long as a $300 minimum balance is maintained. The cost of maintaining this balance will depend upon how much you could earn on the $300 if it was elsewhere. Assume you feel you would be able to earn an 8% after-tax return, or $24 per year. This indicates that you should be maintaining the minimum balance (an annual cost of $24 vs.

$32) and that joining the bank club should be viewed in an even more unfavorable light.

Before you become a club member figure out exactly which of the services you would normally buy and what each would cost. Then compare the result with the cost of joining the bank club. Do not forget that it is often possible to obtain some of the services without charge at other institutions. For example, if you are a member of a credit union, you may already be able to purchase travelers checks without a fee.

24. Check on Financial Aid
If You Have Children Nearing College Age

If you have a son or daughter approaching college age, you are probably terrified at the thought of what a little more education is going to cost. If they are in college now, you already know the bad news. Like nearly everything else, the cost of a college education is going up. Tuition is higher, books cost more, and room and board are out of sight. Do not despair too much, however, for there may be some help available.

As college costs have risen, financial aid has proliferated. And although many of the programs continue to be based upon need, there are some types of aid not tied to financial status. Even for aid programs where need must be demonstrated, family income is not the only factor taken into consideration. For example, family size, unusual family expenses, number of children in school, and amount of family assets are also typically considered. In addition, there are several different systems for determining need, so that the variables are not always evaluated in the same way. It is quite possible that a person might qualify for financial aid without realizing it.

So where do you get started? A first step is to call a toll-free hotline (800-638-6700; 800-492-6602 in Maryland) to the Federal Student Information Center for Financial Aid. Here you can obtain information on programs administered by the Department of Education and may be referred to other potential sources of financial aid that are provided for your particular case. You should also ask for the *Student Consumer's Guide*, a free 19-page booklet that describes six popular federal financial aid programs for college students. You may also obtain a copy by writing Consumer Information Center, Pueblo, Colorado 81009. The booklet includes information on how much you can get and how to apply, when to apply, and how to find out if you qualify for such popular programs as Basic Education Opportunity Grants, National Direct Student Loans, and Guaranteed Student Loans. It also includes information on a loan program for medical and dental school.

For someone who is already in college or who has narrowed down his or her choices to a few schools, it is always worthwhile to visit the financial aid office of a college. Good financial aid officers are worth their weight in gold to both the colleges and the students. They will be familiar with federal programs as well as available state and private financial aid. Most colleges, especially the private ones, have endowments and special scholarships to attract students. Depending upon an individual student's needs, a college will normally assemble a package of aid which is drawn from a number of programs.

Most important, make the effort to find aid. If you do not search, you will never know if you qualify or not. And be sure to start early enough or you might find out too late.

25. Consider Cost of Living
in Deciding upon a Place to Live

Your boss just told you the good news: your promotion was approved and you have an opportunity to transfer to Indianapolis at a higher salary. Or maybe a competing firm in New Orleans called last night and offered you a new position that offers a significant increase in income. Perhaps you are near graduation and have job offers from companies in Atlanta, Houston, Minneapolis, and Seattle. What should you do?

Although your ultimate decision will rest upon a number of factors, including future promotion possibilities, climate, family ties, cultural amenities, and city size, one of the most important considerations should be the cost of living. Living costs vary widely from city to city and from one region of the country to another. In fact, the disparities in living costs are often so great that a promotion resulting in a higher monetary income that requires that you relocate in another city may actually result in a lower real income (i.e., monetary income adjusted for price changes) because the cost of living in the new location is so much higher. Never decide upon a place to live without first investigating the expected living costs.

Living costs consist of many different variables, including food, housing, transportation, clothing, personal items, medical expenses, and taxes. Some cities have high prices in some areas but are competitive in others. For example, people in Milwaukee pay relatively high prices for housing and clothing, but relatively low prices for food, transportation, and medical care. On the other hand, residents of Los Angeles have relatively high costs in the areas of housing, transportation, and medical expenses, but lower-than-average costs for clothing, personal care items, and food eaten at home. Some urban areas allow lower personal spending for most consumer goods and services. These include Dayton, Indianapolis, St. Louis, Nashville, and Orlando, Florida. Cities with a relatively high cost of living include Washington, San Francisco, New York, and Boston.

Living costs vary among regions of the country and between metropolitan and nonmetropolitan areas. Among regions, the southern and north-central states generally provide a lower cost of living, while the Northeast and West are most expensive. As you are probably aware, it typically costs considerably more to live in a metropolitan area—especially with respect to expenditures for rent, housing, and taxes.

Before accepting a transfer or a new job, look into a comparison of living costs between your present location and your potential new area. Consider the manner in which you live and attach greater importance to those areas of spending that tend to absorb most of your income. For example, if you are a type of person that likes to spend spare time at home, the cost of housing may be of paramount importance.

Where can you find comparative living costs for various urban areas? Each spring the Department of Labor publishes a lower, intermediate, and higher budget estimate for four-person families living in forty urban areas and regional nonmetropolitan areas around the country. The budgets are calculated for various types of expenditures on the basis of both dollars and a comparative index. For a free copy call 202-272-5060 or write Bureau of Labor Statistics, United States Department of Labor, Washington, D.C. 20212, and ask for the latest *Urban Family Budgets*.

chapter four

Stretching tax dollars

26. Make Out Your Own Tax Return

One of the best ways to save money on your taxes is to make out your own tax return. Of course, there are exceptions, since some people have such complicated income and financial transactions that they need expert tax advice. However, if you are an average person that leads a relatively simple life, learning to complete your own tax return should not be too difficult and it will pay dividends.

The savings here are actually twofold. First, you will save because you do not have to pay a commercial preparer to do the job for you. Second, and much more important, as you learn to calculate your own taxes, you will also learn the ins and outs of the tax laws so that you can take advantage of them. For example, you should learn what types of expenses are deductible and what expenses are not so that you can make expenditures more intelligently. You will know your income tax bracket so that you can make financial decisions correctly (e.g., exactly how much in taxes will you save if you attend the convention?). You will learn how stock and bond investments are taxed.

The alternative to preparing your own taxes is to pay someone to do it for you. One of the problems here is that the person you pay is really restricted by the information you are able to supply. If you do not understand the tax laws, it is almost a sure bet that the information you supply will be less than perfect. And since a taxpayer must have supporting documents to claim deductions, even if the preparer informs you of possible deductions, it may be too late to claim them for the current year. You should also consider one other fact that may be the most important of all: the person you pay to prepare your taxes may not know a great deal more about taxes than you do.

So if you have never calculated your own taxes, how do you get started? First, pick up some tax forms (1040, 1040A, and Schedule A to get started) and the free booklet *Your Federal Income Tax* at your local Internal Revenue Service office. If there is no office nearby, call the toll-free IRS number in the telephone directory (look under "United States Government") and request that the forms be sent to you. You can often find publications concerning income taxes in the local library. These are generally in the form of paperback self-help books that are published annually. You might also try personal finance books since most of these devote a chapter to income taxes. Another possible source of help is a local educational institution that may provide a free or low-cost course in income tax preparation.

Once you have some general familiarity with the forms and the procedures for completing them, engage in some practice runs using your last year's income. When you are ready to start on your current taxes do your best and then take the information to a commercial preparer or the Internal Revenue Service. The IRS will calculate your taxes for free if your income is $20,000 or less ($40,000 if married) and consists only of wages, salaries, tips, interest, dividends, pensions, and annuities. Now check your calculations with those of the preparer. Once you get your feet wet you are on your way and can soon leave the preparer behind.

27. Make Financial Decisions on the Basis of Your Marginal Income Tax Rate

The federal government and many state governments have their income taxes set up to be progressive. That is, the rates are structured so that as your taxable income increases, you must pay a higher percentage of that income in income taxes. The percentage of extra income that you must pay in income taxes is known as your *marginal tax rate* or more popularly as your *tax bracket*. Thus, a person that has a 30% marginal tax rate is said to be in the 30% tax bracket.

To understand how the marginal tax rate is calculated, let us use an example. Suppose that your gross income is $13,000 but that after you adjust this for deductions and exemptions you have a taxable income of $10,000. The federal tax on this is $1,800. Next year your employer gives you a $1,200 raise which results in a $1,000 increase in taxable income and an income tax of $2,050. Your marginal tax rate is calculated as:

Gross Income	Taxable Income	Tax	Extra Tax
$13,000	$10,000	$1,800	–
14,200	11,000	2,050	$250

$$\text{Marginal tax rate} = \frac{\text{extra tax}}{\text{extra taxable income}} = \frac{\$250}{\$1,000} = 25\%$$

It is this marginal tax rate that should always be used in making financial decisions. For example, suppose you are considering attending a professional meeting and that the expenses incurred are permitted as deductions to reduce your taxable income. If you estimate that the cost will be $800 and you have a marginal tax rate of 25%, then you will reduce your income tax bill by $200 (25% of $800) because you spend the $800. Thus, the true cost of attending the meeting is $600, not $800. The same kind of reasoning should be applied in evaluating any expenditure or extra income that affects your income tax bill. Because marginal tax rates rise fairly rapidly as taxable income increases (the top rate is 50%), individuals are finding themselves shoved into higher and higher tax brackets. Knowing your marginal rate is thus very important. To calculate your marginal tax rate follow this procedure:

A. Compute your taxable income.
B. Calculate the income tax on this income.
C. Add $100 to the income in A.
D. Calculate the income tax for the amount in C.
E. Find the amount of the increased tax.
F. Divide the increased tax in E by $100—this is your marginal tax rate.

Also keep in mind that most deductions allowed in computing federal income taxes are also permitted in calculating state income taxes, so that your overall tax bracket may be slightly higher than that which is figured above.

28. Understand the Difference between
Adjustments and Deductions on Your Income Taxes

Most people know that they are allowed to subtract certain expenses from their income in calculating income taxes for a year. For example, a person should keep track of such things as interest paid on a home mortgage, charitable contributions, and medical expenses. Then, when income taxes are being calculated, if all of these expenses amount to more than a fixed amount that is allowed (called the *zero bracket amount*), a taxpayer should choose the path of itemizing deductions.

Fewer people know that certain expenses, called *adjustments*, can be subtracted from income even if the taxpayer does not have many itemized deductions and chooses the zero bracket amount. In a simple sketch, the

Gross income	$ xxx.xx
less: Adjustments	xxx.xx
Adjusted gross income	$ xxx.xx
less: Itemized deductions or zero bracket amount	xxx.xx
less: Exemptions (e.g., dependents)	xxx.xx
Taxable income	$ xxx.xx

Thus, for individuals who do not have many deductions, adjustments are quite valuable because they can be used in addition to the full amount of the zero bracket amount in reducing taxable income. For a person who has many deductible expenses, for practical purposes, an adjustment is the same as other itemized deductions. Since the adjustments that are allowed are relatively limited in number, it is worthwhile listing and briefly describing them.

1. Moving Expenses. If your new job meets certain requirements, you may deduct most of the reasonable expenses, including temporary living expenses, cost of a mover, premove househunting expenses, etc.

2. Employees' Expenses. An employee who has travel, entertainment, and gift expenses in connection with his or her employment may be able to deduct the cost if they are documented and not reimbursed.

3. Payments to IRA and Keogh Retirement Plans. If you are eligible for one of these plans and make a contribution within the established limits, you may deduct the annual contribution as an adjustment.

4. Interest Penalty on Early Savings Withdrawal. If you have a savings certificate and need to withdraw your funds prior to maturity, you may deduct the penalty that is charged.

5. Alimony. You may deduct alimony, separate maintenance, or similar periodic payments that you are required to make to your spouse or former spouse. This does not include payments for child support.

6. Disability Income Payments. You may generally deduct up to $5,200 (1979) of your disability payments annually if you qualify for the disability income exclusion.

29. Don't Overlook Those Often-Overlooked Tax Deductions

Taxpayers are permitted to reduce their taxable income if they make certain types of expenditures during the year. Some of the best-known deductions include interest payments, charitable contributions, the cost of drugs and doctors (within limits), and tax payments to state and local governments (on federal tax returns). If the sum of all these deductions exceeds a minimum amount that is allowed by the government, then the taxpayer will minimize his or her tax liability by maximizing the amount of deductions that can be found. As a result, it is in every taxpayer's interest to be aware of what deductions are available. Some of those that are overlooked are:

1. Medical payment coverage that is carried as part of your automobile insurance if the cost is reasonable and if the coverage is identifiable and listed separately on your insurance contract (or billed separately.

2. Vitamins that are prescribed or recommended by your doctor.

3. Contributions of property to a charity at their fair market value.

4. Damage to trees and shrubs on residential property that results in a casualty loss. Possible causes are wind, flood, and fire. Losses from disease are not allowed.

5. Local sales taxes which many times are not included in the optional sales tax table in your tax packet. The sales tax table generally includes only the part of the tax that is statewide. Also remember that sales tax payments on big purchases (such as an automobile) are in addition to what the table shows.

6. Education expenses that maintain or improve skills required in your present work or that are required by your employer. These include books, tuition, and driving to and from class.

7. The cost of false teeth, hearing aids, and eyeglasses.

8. Employment agency fees and other expenses you have in seeking new employment in the same trade or business. If the job involves a new trade or business the costs are not deductible.

9. Trade and professional magazines related to your work.

10. Rental for a safe-deposit box that is used for the storage of stocks, bonds, or investment-related papers and documents.

11. Use of your motor vehicle for assisting a qualified charitable organization. You may deduct actual out-of-pocket expenses (excluding depreciation and repairs) or a standard mileage rate (9 cents a mile in 1980).

30. Bunch Tax Deductions

As mentioned elsewhere in this book, the federal government allows taxpayers to reduce their taxable income if they make expenditures that fall into certain categories. Examples include interest, charitable contributions, state and local taxes, medical expenses, and professional publications. By April 15, you tally up all these expenditures you have made in the prior year and subtract the sum from your adjusted gross income on your way to calculating taxable income.

If you do not keep track of these expenditures or if you do not have very many of them, the government allows you to deduct a certain amount in place of itemizing deductions. This amount, called the zero bracket amount, is set by Congress and has been periodically increased.

For the 1980 tax year, single persons and heads of households could claim $2,300, married persons filing jointly (on the same form) and qualifying widows and widowers were allowed $3,400, and married persons filing separately could deduct $1,700 each. Consequently, if a married couple filing jointly could not come up with at least $3,400 in itemized deductions during 1980, they were allowed to claim the zero bracket amount of $3,400.

In most instances, individual taxpayers are on a cash basis and must claim deductions in the year when actual payments are made. For example, if you visit a doctor in December 1981, but do not pay the doctor's bill until the following month, you can only claim the deduction for the 1982 tax year. Likewise, if you pledge a charitable contribution during one year, but do not actually send a check to the charity until the following year, you can only itemize this deduction for the second year. Of course, it is also possible to prepay certain items, and again you will take the deduction in the year when payment is made. One exception to this rule is that you are not allowed to prepay interest and take the entire payment as a deduction in the year of the payment. You may deduct in each year only the interest that belongs to that year.

Now it becomes easier to see how payment dates can be altered to take advantage of the zero bracket amount. If you are a person who is borderline between itemizing and taking the zero bracket amount, you should do one during one year and the other during the next year. Try to concentrate deductible expenditures during the year you choose to itemize. Many expenditures entail quite a lot of flexibility as to time so as to allow you to legally take maximum advantage of the tax laws. Then, during the following year when you have few itemized deductions, you can take the zero bracket amount.

31. Take Advantage of the
Annual Gift Exclusion to Reduce Estate Taxes

You probably think your assets do not amount to enough so that your estate will be taxed at your death. You may be right. Then again, you may be dead wrong by underestimating both the potential size of your estate and the greed of your government.

The federal estate tax was substantially altered in the Tax Reform

Act of 1976. The change was prompted by persistent inflation which had pushed the monetary value of many families' assets to the point that federal estate taxes were taking big chunks of money from more and more estates—especially those involving family farms. What Congress did was to increase the size to which an estate could grow before it would be taxed and to increase the amount that could be left to a spouse free of taxes. However, the new law also made it more difficult to reduce estate taxes through large gifts.

Basically, what the new law allows is a tax-free estate of approximately $250,000 after estate administration expenses (funeral expenses, legal fees, etc.), charitable bequests, and a marital deduction (if married).

Thus, it is quite possible that your estate will be sufficiently small to escape taxation. However, remember that your house, life insurance policies, and securities may amount to significantly more than you think. Also be aware that once your estate passes through the tax-free barrier, the tax rate escalates rapidly. For example, if you leave any assets over those outlined above, the minimum tax rate is 18%. And that is just for starters on the first $10,000. If your estate amounts to $100,000 more than the tax-free allotment, the tax will be $23,800. At $250,000, the tax jumps to $70,800. The more you leave, the higher the rate at which it is taxed.

One way to reduce this tax bill is to give away some assets prior to your death. Not a lot, for the new tax law did away with the lower tax rate on gifts by unifying large gifts with the amount of an estate for tax purposes. However, it is still possible to give away up to $10,000 annually and not have the gift subject to federal taxation. And you may give up to $10,000 to as many individuals for as many years as you wish. If you are married, your spouse may do likewise. If you have four children (although the recipients do not have to be relatives), you may give each an annual gift of $10,000. Assuming your spouse does the same, the two of you are able to transfer $80,000 of assets out of your estate every year. If you have a large estate, these gifts could result in significant tax savings. There is one catch: any gifts you make in the three years prior to your death will be included in your estate anyway. Those feds just don't let a sleeping dog lie.

32. If You Plan to Leave Part of Your Estate
to Charity, Consider Making Donations Now

Many individuals make plans to leave all or a portion of their assets to a charitable organization when they die. For example, a person may stipulate in her will that, at her death, $50,000 be given to Parrishe University to establish a scholarship fund for disadvantaged youths from Rushville, Indiana. Or an individual may decide to leave all his stock in Howell Brothers Corporation to his church. Although these bequests are surely made because the donor believes the charities are deserving and pursue worthy goals, there is a very definite tax advantage involved. Property that is passed to a qualified charitable organization is exempt from estate taxes. For example, if you specify in your will that $10,000 of your estate be given to a qualified charity, that $10,000 will not be included in your taxable estate at your death. There is no limit to the portion of an estate that can be left to a charitable organization.

If you plan to leave part of your estate to a charity, you will be able to increase the tax benefits by actually making the gift prior to your death. The reason is that gifts to qualified charitable organizations can be used to reduce personal income taxes so long as they do not exceed 50% of adjusted gross income. Thus, a gift to charity while you are alive will reduce your personal income taxes in the year in which the gift is made, and since you no longer own the property, the asset will not be a part of your estate for estate tax purposes.

To see how this works, suppose you are widowed and have accumulated a significant amount of assets that you plan to leave mostly to your children with $20,000 to go to a favorite charity. The $20,000 will not be included in your taxable estate, and it is estimated that this will result in reduced estate taxes of $8,000. Let us also assume that you are still working and have an annual income which puts you in the 45% marginal income tax bracket (the percentage of every extra dollar of taxable income that must be paid in income taxes). If you decide to eliminate the $20,000 bequest from your will, and instead give the money to the charity now, your income tax bill for the year will be reduced by 45% of $20,000, or $9,000. You can spend the $9,000 savings on an around-the-world trip and the charity and your children will be just as well off as if you had left the gift in your will rather than giving it now. And who suffers because of your change in plans? The government, since its tax revenues are reduced.

33. Make Charitable Contributions with Property That Has Appreciated in Value

Have you been making annual contributions of cash to your church, the United Way, the Sierra Club, or your alma mater? If you have, you may have also been missing one of the best tax gimmicks around. A major incentive for making a charitable gift is that it allows you to reduce taxable income and, as a result, your income tax liability if you normally itemize deductions. However, there is another potential tax break which allows you to magnify the tax savings if you make the right kind of gift. Yes, Virginia, there is a tax-loophole Santa for the ordinary person.

The federal government allows an individual to make contributions of property as well as money and still receive the tax benefit of a charitable gift. The loophole to this stems from the fact that you are permitted to contribute property which has appreciated in value since the time you acquired it, and yet escape taxation on the gain. Suppose you purchased securities years ago and they have since appreciated greatly in value. If you give the securities to a qualifying charity, you may take the full current value of the gift as an itemized deduction on your income tax, but perhaps not be subject to any taxation on the gain in value which has occurred.

In order better to understand the tax advantage from this, let us use a hypothetical example. Assume you purchase 50 shares of American Telephone & Telegraph common stock in 1970 for $40 per share, or a total outlay of $2,000. In 1982, your church asks that you contribute a sizable sum to its building fund. If AT&T stock has since gone up in price to $60 per share, you may give your shares to the church and receive a deduction for the full $3,000. At the same time, you are able to escape paying income taxes on the long-term gain of $1,000 (i.e., $3,000 current value less $2,000 cost basis). If you are in the 30% marginal income tax bracket, this would mean an additional savings of $120, since only 40% of a long-term gain is taxable at a taxpayer's ordinary tax rate. As a general rule, you receive this favorable treatment on property whose sale would result in a long-term (held over one year) capital gain, but there are exceptions. One such exception is tangible personal property (e.g., art or antiques) that is unrelated to the donee organization's exempt function. As an example, giving a work of art to a youth activity organization would not qualify. However, a similar gift to a museum would be a different story. You should be aware that there are maximum limits on the amount you may give and deduct in any one year, even if the gifts are in cash.

As you can probably tell, the tax laws here are somewhat complicated, so you should probably discuss your proposed gift with a tax attorney prior to reaching a decision on a charitable contribution. However, the tax advantages of making a charitable gift of appreciated property, rather than money, can be so great that it is worth your time and money to investigate the possibility. Happy loopholes.

chapter five

Stretching
investment income

34. Transfer Income-Producing Property to Minors

A good method of increasing your after-tax investment return is to transfer a portion of your income to someone else—specifically, dependents who may pay little or no tax on the income. Of course, you cannot transfer just the income, you must actually transfer the property that produces the income. The idea is to move income from a person being taxed at a high rate (you) to a person being taxed at a low rate (your child). This maneuver makes a great deal of sense if you are investing a portion of your income for a child's benefit anyway.

Suppose you have decided to establish a fund that will be used to pay for your newly born daughter's college education. Let us assume your salary and investment income place you in the 30% tax bracket so that you have to pay 30 cents of every additional dollar of income to the federal and state governments. If you find yourself able to place $4,000 in a savings certificate that earns 10% annually, the after-tax return will actually be 7.0% (70% of 10%). Such a return will result in your accumulating $13,520 in the fund by the time your daughter is ready for college in 18 years. However, if you and your spouse give the $4,000 to your infant daughter and place the money in the same savings certificate, she will not have to pay any taxes on the interest income, so that the fund will accumulate to $22,240 by the time 18 years have passed. Thus, by transferring the initial $4,000 to your daughter, the fund for college will earn an additional $8,720 of after-tax income (assuming she will not have to pay any taxes during these years). You should be aware that there is an annual gift limitation of $10,000 ($20,000 if given by both husband and wife) to any one recipient before it is necessary to concern yourself about the possibility of gift taxes.

Gifts made to children in this manner are allowed under the Uniform Gifts to Minors Acts. It is important to understand that the gifts must be of a permanent nature (i.e., you may not take the money back when you see fit) and the proceeds may not be utilized to pay for things that you are legally obligated to provide anyway (e.g., food and shelter). In addition, when your daughter turns 18 years old, she takes possession of the $22,240 and may use it as she desires. Prior to her turning 18, however, you are able to control the gift and the income it generates as custodian of the fund. Any bank, savings and loan association, or brokerage house can provide you with the relatively simple details of opening such an account.

35. Use a Discount Broker for Securities Transactions

Since 1975 securities brokerage firms have been permitted to compete for customers on the basis of fees. Beginning in May of that year, brokers moved from a period when commissions were fixed to an era of negotiable rates. Actually, rates are still not negotiable for any but the largest investors. Still, it is now possible to save on brokerage commissions by shopping around, since not all companies charge the same fees.

After the fixed-fee schedule was eliminated, brokerage firms began to congregate into one of two categories. Most of the large well-known firms such as Paine Webber, Dean Witter, Thomson McKinnon, E. F. Hutton, Merrill Lynch, and Bache continued to offer a full line of services at many offices around the country. Nearly all these companies now charge commissions that are higher than the fixed rates that existed in 1975.

At the opposite end of the spectrum are an increasing number of discount brokerage firms. These companies typically offer little or no investment advice and operate out of a single office that may be reached by means of a toll-free telephone number. Their lower overhead (fewer brokers, few offices, no research) allows these firms to charge one-half or less (with a $25 to $35 minimum) what the full-line companies charge for identical trades. There are currently over a hundred discount brokerage companies in operation.

Since not all discount firms charge the same commissions or offer the same services, you may want to compare a number of firms before deciding if and where to open an account. Nearly any issue of the *Wall Street Journal* or *Barron's* will contain a number of advertisements with toll-free numbers to call for requesting information packets. To get started you might try:

- Quick & Reilly (800-221-5220)—one of the best-known.
- Charles Schwab & Co. (800-227-4444)—one of the biggest.
- Kashner Lodge Securities (800-237-9631)—low minimum fee.
- Discount Brokerage Corporation (800-221-5088)—low commission.
- Source Securities (800-221-5338)—one of the oldest.

It is important to realize that discount brokerage firms are designed for individuals who make their own investment decisions. These individuals may make their decisions on the basis of reading advisory services such as the *Value Line Investment Survey* or *Standard & Poor's Outlook* (both available in many libraries). Perhaps they use their own research or the advice of friends. For investors who rely on brokerage recommendations, using a discount broker is a questionable decision. One compromise is to open one account with a discounter and another with a full-line firm and spread business between the two.

If you are interested in additional information on discount brokers, look for the November/December 1980 issue of *Business* (published by Georgia State University, College of Business Administration, Atlanta, Georgia 30303) in a library. It contains an article, "Discount Brokers: Less Advice at a Better Price," that provides a comparison of the commissions charged by twenty-two discount firms. It also examines the evolution of this segment of the industry.

36. If You Qualify, Take Advantage of an Individual Retirement Account

If you think Congress initiates tax breaks and loopholes only for the rich, you are wrong. Not by much, of course, but there is a bone that Congress has thrown to middle-income taxpayers in order to encourage them to put aside funds for their own retirement. This is the Individual Retirement Account, or as it is more popularly known, the IRA. Individual Retirement Accounts were established to allow a wage earner to set aside a portion of his or her income and take a tax deduction for the amount of the contribution.

There is one very good reason to take advantage of an IRA if you are eligible—the tax benefit. Suppose you earn $30,000 per year and pay taxes at a rate of 30% on your top income. As discussed elsewhere in this book, the 30% is known as your *tax bracket* or *marginal tax rate* (see number 27). If you are able to set aside $1,000 each year free of income taxes, you will reduce your tax bill in that year by $300 (30% of $1,000). If you pay income taxes at a rate of 35%, your tax bill will be reduced by $350. Not only is your tax bill reduced in the year of your contribution, but the income that these contributions earn does not have to be reported. There is a catch. You will have to pay income taxes on all the money that you eventually withdraw from your IRA, so it is really a case of deferring income taxes rather than avoiding them altogether. Most individuals will be in a lower income tax bracket at the time of their retirement, so the tax bite on the withdrawal will not be so large.

There are some restrictions to an IRA with which you should be familiar. The maximum contribution in any one year is $2,000. There is currently talk of raising these limits, so you may want to check with a local financial institution or the Internal Revenue Service to see if any changes are applicable to your particular case. Another important restriction on IRAs is that withdrawals cannot be made without a severe penalty prior to age 59½ and withdrawals must commence before age 70½. Be aware that you cannot use an IRA as collateral for a loan and you are not permitted to borrow against it.

There are a number of ways to establish an Individual Retirement Account. These include putting funds into savings accounts at financial institutions, annuities sold mainly by life insurance companies, mutual funds, and trusts administered by financial institutions. There is no reason you have to put all your contribution into a single plan, and it is important to understand that you are allowed to move your funds from one plan to another every three years. Be wary of plans that have high front-end sales charges or that require annual fixed payments. Both of these apply primarily to annuities sold by insurance companies. You might consider putting half into high-yielding certificates in a financial institution and half into a mutual fund (watch for a sales charge).

For additional information on IRAs, call (toll-free) or write the IRS and ask for Publication 590, *Individual Retirement Arrangements.*

37. Do Not Invest in Preferred Stock

Preferred stock is issued by corporations in order to raise long-term funds for expansion and the replacement of assets. While retention of earnings and the sale of common stock and bonds are used to a greater extent, preferred stock still represents an important source of money to many corporations—especially utilities—and the shares are available for individuals to purchase.

Preferred stock is a type of security that pays a constant-dollar dividend to its holder. The size of the dividend is fixed at the time the security is originally sold by the company and is not changed while the shares remain outstanding regardless of how many times they are traded among investors. That is, the dividend is not supposed to change. Like payments to common stockholders, dividends to preferred stockholders must be voted on by a corporation's directors, so there is always the possibility that a dividend may be omitted. However, nearly all issues of preferred are of a type called *cumulative,* so that if the dividend is not paid on time, it must be made up at a later date before any dividend may be paid to common stockholders. Preferred stockholders not only have a preference over the company's common stockholders with respect to dividends, they also have preference with respect to a claim against assets in the event the company is liquidated. Like common stock issues, preferred stocks carry no maturity date on which the stockholders have the principal amount of their securities returned.

Preferred stock is a hybrid security that has some of the characteristics of bonds and some of those of common stocks. Actually, it has the worst aspects of each. Like bonds, its annual payments are fixed so that a preferred stockholder cannot participate in a firm's growth. Like common stockholders, a preferred holder has no specified date on which a specific amount of money will be returned. In addition, in the event the firm gets into trouble, the position of the preferred stockholder is much less secure than that of a bondholder in the same company, but not much better than that of common stockholders.

Preferred stockholders are subject to the risks that interest rates will rise and that the issuer will go broke. Although common stockholders have these same risks, their potential rewards are much greater. The moral is that if you are interested in a fixed and relatively secure income, you should buy bonds. If you desire growth and large potential price gains, buy common stock.

38. Avoid Buying Mutual Funds That Charge a Sales Fee

A mutual fund is a firm that invests in the stocks and bonds of other companies in order to earn a return for its owners. In other words, while many business firms acquire factories and/or equipment in order to produce a product that can be sold to the public, mutual funds invest their owners' funds in the securities of businesses (and sometimes governments). Some of these mutual funds specialize in certain types of securities (stocks of growth companies or municipal bonds, for example), while others accumulate a variety of stocks and bonds (called *balanced funds*). Some funds try to earn a high current return for their owners, and other investment companies select securities that offer a promise of long-term appreciation but little current return.

The shares of mutual funds are sold in two ways. Some funds offer their shares directly to the public at what is termed the *net asset value*. This is just the total value of securities held by the fund divided by the number of shares of ownership it has outstanding. If an investment company holds $1,000,000 worth of securities and has 100,000 of its own shares outstanding, the net asset value will be $10 per share. This is the price that would be charged for new shares. Of course, if the value of the securities held by a mutual fund increases or decreases, the net asset value of its own shares will change. Mutual funds that sell shares at net asset value are called *no-load funds*.

Another group of mutual funds sell their shares to the public through salespersons such as stockbrokers. These funds operate in the same manner as the no-load funds just discussed except they are sold at prices of 7 to 9% greater than their net asset value with the difference (called the loading charge) going to the salesperson. For example, if you put $1,000 into the shares of one of these funds, you will actually receive shares valued at only $920 or $930. It should be stated that while loading charges of 7 to 9% are most common, some funds charge commissions that are less.

There is no reason to believe that funds which employ a salesperson should perform better than funds that sell their shares directly to the public. After all, it is not the sales staff that selects the securities in which a fund invests. The result is that loading fees paid to acquire shares of mutual funds are wasted dollars as far as consumers are concerned. Stay away from mutual funds that sell shares at a price greater than net asset value.

Remember that all mutual funds charge a management fee. To check on the size of a particular fund's fees and past performance, go to the library and look at the annual report on investment companies in each year's late-August edition of *Forbes* magazine.

chapter six

Stretching borrowing dollars

39. When You Borrow, Check the APR

Suppose you find a lender that will loan you $200 and charge only $10 in interest. Is the cost of borrowing the money 5% ($10/$200)? Perhaps. It depends on a number of things, including: (1) When does the loan have to be repaid? (2) Is the loan repaid in a lump sum at some future date, or do you make a series of installment payments? (3) Is the $10 in interest subtracted from the amount of the loan so that you actually receive only $190?

As you may be aware, there are a variety of methods available for calculating interest and stating interest rates—so many, in fact, that a large number of borrowers really have no idea what rates they are paying so that they are unable to compare quoted rates among lenders. One lender might quote a lower rate than another lender even though the cost of borrowing is actually higher. The reason, of course, is that there are so many different ways to quote the rate of interest on the same loan.

In an effort to remedy this problem, Congress passed the Consumer Credit Protection Act in 1968. Under this act, a lender is required to tell you—in writing and before you sign any agreement—two valuable pieces of information that will allow you to compare the cost of credit from different sources. The first is the total dollar amount of the finance charge (including interest and sometimes other costs such as a service charge) you will pay to use credit. In other words, how many dollars will you have to repay that are in addition to the amount you borrow? The second, and more important disclosure, is that the lender must quote you the annual percentage rate (APR) on the loan. This standardized rate is a relative measure of the cost of credit on an annual basis (even if the loan is for a period other than a year), and knowing it allows you to compare lenders.

Remember, all creditors—finance companies, car dealers, banks, and credit card companies—must supply you with these two pieces of information before a contract is finalized. Although you may want to include some other items in your decision as to where to borrow (does one lender require credit life insurance, for example?), as a general rule you should choose the one offering the lowest APR unless there is some particular reason to do otherwise. For more information on credit protection write Publications Services, Division of Administrative Services, Board of Governors of the Federal Reserve System, Washingto, D.C. 20551 and ask for the free 46-page publication, *Consumer Handbook to Credit Protection Laws.*

40. Tear up Your Credit Cards

Would you believe me if I told you I just came home wearing a new suit, bought a gift for my wife, had a new set of tires put on my car, and yet didn't have any money with me when I left home this morning? I didn't have to write a check either (our balance was too low anyway). Now you see!! Sure, I just paid in plastic. If you pay in plastic, you leave all your worries behind. Well, maybe we should say ahead.

For many individuals this plastic (better known as the credit card) brings a little extra convenience at a very high price. The conveniences are actively promoted and well known. They include not having to carry a lot of money, finding it easier to cash checks, having a record of expenditures for expense accounts or tax records, and being able to acquire items without having to pay for them until a later date.

Perhaps the greatest single drawback of having credit cards is that you will tend to buy things you ordinarily would pass up. To a large extent this stems from the fact that you do not have to pay (or even have) any real money at the time a purchase is made so that the pleasure of acquiring something is not immediately matched by the pain of paying. It is much like the feeling you have when gambling with casino chips in Reno. After a time a person begins to view the chips as something other than money, so the pain of losing is not so great. If it is necessary to pull money out of a wallet or purse every time a bet is placed, a string of losses hits home fast. Likewise, if you are forced to pull out your wallet or write a check and look at your new balance every time you purchase something, the actual cost is quite evident.

The best-known disadvantage of using credit cards is the higher price you end up paying because of interest charges. In some cases interest is not added unless a user fails to pay on the first billing date after a purchase. However, lenders have been tending to change this by charging interest from the date a purchase is made. This change increases the interest cost and makes it impossible to use the lender's money without being charged. The minimum interest rate charged by most issuers of credit cards is 18%. The net effect of this is that credit card users find the cost of goods they purchase to be higher with the result that they have less money for other things.

A lesser-known disadvantage of credit card use is that it tends to increase the cost of goods for all consumers. Credit card issuers try to make money from businesses that accept credit cards as payment, as well as from consumers that use credit cards. The charge to an individual business will be figured as a percentage of the amount charged. Thus, if you pay for a restaurant meal by slipping the cashier some plastic, the restaurant owner might well have to pay 4 or 5% of the bill to the credit card company. The result is that the owner will tend to raise menu prices to cover the additional cost.

So why not try a recipe for financial health? Take out all of your credit cards, cut each one into sixteen equal pieces, mix them all carefully together, and then deposit the result in the round file. You may think it is impossible to live in today's world without using credit cards. It is not.

41. If You Must Borrow,
Try Your Life Insurance Policy

If you feel that you must borrow money, there will be few places where you can obtain it more cheaply than from the insurance company that sold you a life insurance policy—that is, if you bought the kind of life insurance that allows this type of loan and if you have been paying on the policy long enough.

Life insurance companies sell two major types of policies—term and ordinary. Term is often called *pure* or *protection-only insurance* since it is possible to collect only if the insured dies. No savings, no payment at retirement, and nothing if you decide to cancel. There is nothing wrong with owning this type of policy and, in fact, many experts prefer it. The premiums are low but will increase as the insured grows older since an older person is more likely to die in a given year than someone who is younger.

For a variety of reasons, insurance companies also sell a type of insurance called *ordinary insurance* in which the premiums are constant. These unchanging payments are made possible by the fact that the insurance company charges premiums that are considerably higher than the actual cost of insuring a person in the early years of the policy. These funds are invested by the company and the income that is earned is combined with the higher-than-normal premiums to allow the company to offset the higher cost of insurance in the later years of the policy. Over a period of years, these savings build up in a policy and give it something called *cash value.* A policy's cash value will be paid to a policyholder in the event a policy is canceled or may be borrowed against if a loan is desired.

Since cash values build up over time, the longer a given policy has been in force, the greater its cash value and the more that may be borrowed. Cash values will be listed on the policy for selected years of a policy's life, or a policyholder may write the company and inquire about how much may be borrowed. The rate of interest charged on the loan will be set at the time the policy is taken out and will be listed in the policy. In general, the rate is quite low—in the area of 8% on newer policies and 5 to 6% on older policies. It is very doubtful that you can obtain a lower rate anywhere else. The loans are particularly opportune for replacing installment loans for the purchase of such things as cars and large appliances. In fact, it may be to your advantage to borrow against your life insurance and use the proceeds to invest in a certificate of deposit or money market fund that offers a rate higher than that which you are charged.

Although there is no definite time when a loan on a policy must be repaid, it is important to understand that should the insured die while a loan is outstanding, the payment to the beneficiary will be reduced by the amount of the unpaid loan and its unpaid interest.

42. Consider Borrowing against Your
Savings Account for Short-Term Credit Needs

Suppose you need an extra $500 for three weeks. Should you go to the bank or credit union and apply for a personal loan? How about borrowing on the cash value of your life insurance policy? Or maybe you should simply go to the savings and loan association or credit union and withdraw $500 from your savings account. All these alternatives will probably provide you with the needed money, of course, but all of them also present some possible drawbacks.

If you need the money quickly, your insurance policy is out because of the time involved. Securing a loan from the bank or credit union may be accomplished quickly, but you may find that the interest rate is quite high. In addition, some lending institutions charge a service fee that makes the cost of small, short-term loans fairly expensive. Making a temporary withdrawal from your savings account may be a smart thing to do depending upon the type of account you have. If it is a passbook account, with interest figured from the day of deposit to the day of withdrawal, this may be your best bet. On the other hand, if your savings is in the form of a certificate of deposit, you may be penalized for a withdrawal prior to the certificate's maturity. Also, if your account only pays interest semi-annually or quarterly, a withdrawal will result in the loss of interest which has been earned on the withdrawn money since the last interest payment date.

One of the quickest, easiest, and cheapest methods of obtaining a short-term loan is to borrow against the funds in your savings account. These loans, often called *share loans*, are generally allowed against any type of account with the exception of six-month money-market certificates. The interest rate will be determined by the individual institution, but you can expect to pay 2 to 3% more than you are earning on the savings account. Thus, if you have a certificate of deposit paying 7%, you will be able to borrow against the account at a rate of 9 or 10%.

You obviously do not want to obtain funds on a long-term basis in this manner, since you are paying a higher rate than you are receiving. However, for short-term requirements a share loan may be ideal.

43. Take out a 25-Year Rather Than a 30-Year Mortgage

Mortgages on residential property are commonly made as amortized or installment loans. With this type of repayment arrangement the borrower makes fixed payments, with a portion of each payment going to cover interest and the remaining part used to reduce principal (i.e., the amount owed). The size of payments calculated when the loan is made is just enough to reduce the principal to zero on the date the loan is to be paid off. Early in the life of an amortized loan the major part of each payment goes toward covering interest, with only a small portion used for principal reduction. Conversely, when a loan is close to being paid off, nearly all of each payment is used to reduce the principal.

Because of the nature of an amortized loan, if the payments are increased in size, all of the additional amount will reduce the balance of the loan. For example, suppose you take out a 30-year $50,000 mortgage that carries an annual rate of interest of 12.5%. This will require a monthly payment of $533.63 (not including insurance or taxes). When you make your first payment, $520.83 will go to pay the first month's interest and the remaining $12.80 will reduce the principal on the loan. Since you owe $12.80 less during the second month, the interest charge will fall to $520.70 and your $533.63 payment will allow a reduction of principal of $12.93. Now suppose you had decided upon monthly payments of $545.18 rather than $533.63. You would pay the same $520.83 in interest during the first month, but $24.35 would be available for principal reduction. The entire difference between the two payments ($11.55) is utilized to reduce principal. In fact, you would find that if you continued to make the $545.18 payments in place of the $533.60 payments, the loan would be paid off in 25, rather than 30, years. A 20-year payoff on the same loan would require monthly payments of $568.08.

Some financial advisors suggest that potential homeowners negotiate for as long a loan as possible. They argue that a home will be easier to resell if buyers can assume your loan without putting up too much equity (the difference between your asking price and what you owe on the loan). They also say that your home will be appreciating in value while you have locked the lending institution into fixed payments. In any case, the interest portion of each payment is tax-deductible. This is all well and good, but consider the total savings that will result if you take a shorter-term loan. The calculations assume a $50,000 loan at an annual interest rate of 12.5%:

Term	20 years	25 years	30 years
Monthly payment	$568.08	$545.18	$533.63
Number of payments	240	300	360
Total dollars paid	$136,339.20	$163,554.00	$192,106.80
Total interest paid	$86,339.20	$113,554.00	$142,106.80
Extra interest	—	$27,214.80	$55,767.60

44. Avoid Credit Life Insurance

Credit life insurance is issued through a lender as a method of repaying the outstanding balance on a debt in case the borrower dies. In most instances the insurance is simply a term policy with a face value that declines with the loan balance. Such a policy insures that the deceased's estate, and thus his or her heirs, are relieved of paying off the loan. For example, suppose you borrow $10,000 from the local bank in order to buy a new $15,000 sports car (a trade-in is used for the remaining $5,000) and the banker convinces you to buy a credit life policy. After one year of paying on the 4-year loan and bringing the balance down to $8,000, you suddenly die of some strange disease. The credit life policy will pay off the balance of the loan so that the car will be in your estate free and clear of any debt. Had you not taken out the policy, it would be necessary for the person handling your estate to use other funds or perhaps sell the car in order to pay the loan balance.

As a general rule, credit life insurance is an expensive method of obtaining insurance. This is especially true if the borrower is young, since most credit life premiums depend only upon the amount and length of the loan and not the age of the insured. Thus, a 25-year-old and a 50-year-old will end up paying the same price for a credit life policy on loans of similar size and length, even though the true cost of insuring the younger individual is much less. One reason credit life insurance is so expensive is that the lending institution often receives a relatively large portion of the premium paid by the borrower.

Even if credit life insurance were not overpriced, it would be of questionable value. An individual should purchase life insurance based upon his or her overall insurance requirements, not upon the fact that a car or refrigerator was just purchased. If more insurance is needed, the borrower would probably be better advised to use the premium to be charged on credit life as payment toward a larger amount of regular term insurance. In the event the lender requires you to have such a policy, you should investigate the price of decreasing term insurance at an insurance company or consider assigning a life insurance policy you already have to the lending institution. Either of these options should result in a savings to you. Be forewarned that some lending institutions will automatically write credit life into a contract even though they do not require borrowers to accept it. As a result, you should always look for this insertion before you sign on the dotted line.

45. Avoid Financing an Automobile with the Dealer

The easiest method of buying a car is to sit down in the salesperson's office and sign the purchase agreement and installment loan agreement at the same time. You might call it one-stop shopping. Unfortunately, it is also almost surely one of the most expensive ways to finance an automobile purchase. The reason is that dealers typically turn around and sell your contract (at a discount) to a bank or finance company. Most dealers have their hands full financing the cars in their showrooms without worrying about financing the cars of their customers also. Even though the dealers are not actually providing the financing, however, their origination of the loans can prove to be quite profitable. In fact, some dealers make as much or more profit on the loan originations as they do on the actual sales.

If you should not finance an automobile purchase through the dealer, what alternative should you use? The answer is to shop around. First shop for the automobile and then shop for the financing. Different financial institutions charge different rates on car loans. You might initially want to try some banks and see what terms they offer. And you do not even have to appear at the bank in person, since you can find out just as much by telephone. Remember, not all banks charge the same interest rates. An even better course of action may be to check a credit union (if you are a member). Credit unions often offer the lowest rates available on automobile loans. In addition, they generally provide credit life insurance (your loan is automatically paid off in the event you die prior to complete repayment) at no additional charge and allow you to pay off a loan early with no penalty. Another low-cost possibility is to borrow money on your life insurance policy (see number 41).

In summary, here is what you should do:

1. Shop for the car until you feel you have the best deal.

2. Tell the car dealer you will return after finding financing for the car.

3. In order, check on financing by means of (a) your life insurance policy, (b) your credit union, (c) commercial banks.

How much can you expect to save if you shop around? Suppose you need to borrow $6,000 to buy an $8,000 car and decide to repay the loan over a four-year period. Assuming typical annual percentage rates (APR) found below, the total of your 48 payments would be:

Life insurance (@8%)	$7,031
Credit union (@12%)	$7,584
Bank (@14.5%)	$7,943
Dealer (@16%)	$8,162

chapter seven

Stretching insurance dollars

46. Understand the Purpose of Insurance

Every year people probably waste as much money on various types of insurance as they do on any other single product. Not only do they buy the wrong kinds, but they often end up with improper amounts of those types of insurance that should be purchased. The main reason behind this sad state of affairs is that individuals often buy insurance without ever understanding exactly what the policies are designed to accomplish.

Insurance falls into an area of finance known as *risk management*. That is, how can individuals and companies provide for the possibility of a certain type of financial loss? For example, take the case of the possibility of financial loss from damage to an automobile. With respect to the risk of loss you can (a) avoid it (don't own a car), (b) reduce it (drive more carefully or own a car of little value), (c) assume it (pay for damages yourself), or (d) transfer it (buy insurance so someone else pays for the loss). As surprising as it may seem, the last possibility may be the worst method of handling most forms of risk.

Insurance companies are in business to make money or, at worst, break even. The premiums you pay must cover the insurer's administrative costs and policyholders' claims less the returns the companies are able to earn from investments. As a result, over your lifetime, most insurers will pay you less than you pay them. The moral to this is that you should buy only as much insurance as you absolutely require and no more.

And what does a person require? As a general rule, risk should be transferred if the potential loss is too large to handle in any other manner. For example, the potential financial loss from damage to a home is so great that it is almost unthinkable for nearly anyone not to carry a home-owner's policy. A home represents such a huge investment for most individuals that losing it to a fire or tornado would financially break them. Hence, for the vast majority of people, homeowner's insurance is a necessity. The same would be true for automobile liability insurance, which may prevent being financially wiped out because of a lawsuit. Notice that the potential size of a given loss is a more important consideration than the probability of the loss. In fact, smaller losses that occur frequently are almost always better to handle yourself. Perhaps you have an old car worth $400 or $500, for example. Since you can, hopefully, handle this loss without great financial difficulty, it is almost surely in your best interest not to buy collision or comprehensive insurance. Likewise, if you have no dependents, there may be no real financial loss to anyone if you should die prematurely. As a result, purchasing insurance on your life would be a questionable financial decision.

Approach insurance as you would any other product and buy only that which you absolutely require. Any other purchase will generally result in squandering your money. Remember, on an overall basis, insurance tends to be a losing game for most consumers in that they will get less back than they pay in. However, for those potential financial losses that you cannot afford to assume yourself, it is a game you cannot really afford not to play.

47. Shop for Insurance

You have just spent ·a little over two weeks haggling with car dealers before deciding to purchase a brand new automobile. You are quite proud of yourself since you were able to negotiate the price downward by nearly $250 from the dealers' initial quotes. Being the smart shopper that you are, before purchasing the car you called several banks and your credit union in order to obtain a loan at the lowest possible interest cost. Now you merely need to call your insurance company and add the new car to your policy. Wait a minute! You mean you spent all that time and effort in an attempt to save money on the car and its financing, but you are not going to spend a few minutes more to shop for insurance? And you consider yourself a smart shopper?

All insurance companies are not created equal, and neither are the policies they sell. Insurance companies vary in their efficiency, in the types of customers they serve, and in the manner in which they sell their products. Some give multiple-car discounts, new home discounts, or premium reductions for safety features installed in a home. Others have particular aversions to sports cars or young drivers without driver education. The list goes on but the message is clear: premiums may vary widely among insurance companies for what is essentially the same type of coverage.

What this means, of course, is that you should spend a little time shopping for insurance. And do not limit your price shopping to automobile insurance, exclusively. Shop for homeowner's or renter's insurance, floater policies on valuables, liability insurance, health and disability policies, and life insurance. Make sure that you are comparing policies with similar features or the cost comparisons will be misleading. This is particularly difficult with life insurance policies, but for most kinds of insurance, policies are fairly easy to equate.

One of the great advantages of insurance shopping is that nearly all your business can be conducted over the telephone. Another advantage is that, since insurance premiums are a recurring expense, the savings you are able to obtain on the first year's premium will be compounded as you pay premiums in future years. This does not mean that you should never reevaluate the companies with which you do business. Insurance companies do not all raise their premiums by equal amounts each year, so a company that was once a relatively low-cost insurer may become less competitive in its rates over a period of years. However, you should be able to count on at least a few years of below-average rates if you choose the lowest-cost company in the beginning.

If you have found the company with the best rate on an automobile policy, do not automatically assume that this company will also offer the lowest premiums on a homeowner's policy or, especially, a life insurance policy. There are some advantages to buying your insurance through the same company or the same agent (for example, you may have more leverage to get claims settled to your satisfaction), but you should still shop around to see what these advantages are costing you.

48. Use Large Deductibles When Purchasing Insurance

Insurance is a losing game. That is, it is a losing game for consumers—but not, of course, for the companies that sell it. Because of this, you should only insure against financial losses that you cannot handle any other way. One of the best methods of accomplishing this is through the use of deductibles. Actually, this is a form of self-insurance, since you are assuming the risk of the first dollars of loss and transferring the rest to the insurance company. And why should you do such a foolish thing as this? It is simple. The insurance company will charge you lower premiums if you use deductibles than if you require the company to pick up the entire bill for any loss.

Insurance companies set premiums to cover not only the claims they expect to pay, but also the cost to process those claims. You can have your insurance bill reduced by relieving the company of paying those small claims at the same time you can keep your insurance record cleaner by reducing the number of claims you file.

Self-insurance is particularly useful in the purchase of collision and comprehensive insurance on an automobile, homeowner's insurance on a house, disability income insurance (the waiting period is a form of deductible), and major medical insurance. Even though it may irk you to pay insurance premiums and still not be able to file a claim because the loss is too small, in the long run you should benefit from such a policy. Whenever you think otherwise, just stop and remember that insurance companies are not in business to lose money.

It is important that you have sufficient funds available to pay for your share of potential losses or the reduced premiums may be a false economy. If you must borrow the money to pay for the portion of a loss you have self-insured, for example, it is doubtful that you are going to save much from this type of insurance program. As you build up a fund for the purpose of self-insurance it will be possible to increase the size of your deductibles and reduce your premiums more. One partial offset to the possibility that you may be required to cover all or part of a given loss is the fact that the portion of losses above $100 that are not reimbursed by insurance may be used as itemized deductions on your federal income taxes. Thus, the real cost of a loss to you is reduced. The higher your marginal tax rate, the greater the tax savings from a given loss.

How much can you expect to save on your insurance bills by using deductibles? One large insurance company reduces premiums on comprehensive automobile coverage (theft, hail, etc.) about 25% to policyholders who accept $100 deductible rather than full coverage. It also reduces automobile collision premiums about 3% for $100 vs. $50 deductible, 20% for $250 vs. $50 deductible, and 37% for $500 vs. $50 deductible. On a homeowner's policy it charges an additional 2% for policyholders who want a $100 rather than a $250 deductible provision.

49. Buy the Right Kind of Life Insurance

Many individuals purchase a life insurance policy on the basis of the face amount of the policy (how much will be paid to the beneficiary) and the number of years premiums must be paid. They may also have some vague idea of what the contract will be worth (if anything) by the time they are 65 years old. These people buy insurance without ever knowing that a variety of policies are available and that possibly a different type would have been more suitable for their particular needs.

The basic type of life insurance is called *term insurance*. A term policy provides that the beneficiary will receive the face amount of the policy in the event the insured dies while the policy is in force. If you pay on a term policy from age 25 until age 65 then decide to cancel the insurance (quit paying), you will receive nothing, since it will have accumulated no savings. If you die during the following year, there will be no payment to a beneficiary. Term insurance is often described as *pure insurance* because it offers nothing other than payment of face value at the death of the insured.

The other broad category of life insurance is known variously as *ordinary, whole life,* or *cash value insurance.* These policies include fixed premiums throughout the life of a policy (term premiums increase) with a portion of each payment going into savings and a portion paying for the actual insurance. Since a portion of every premium is set aside in savings, these policies can be used for borrowing and they provide holders with a cash payment in case premiums are terminated.

If you think a term policy is inferior to a whole life policy of the same face value, you are probably correct. However, the comparison is really unfair unless you also consider cost. Term policies involve much lower premiums for the same amount of insurance. In other words, you pay the insurance company less and, in turn, the insurance company promises you less.

If a person is young with three or four dependents and little in the way of financial assets, the need for life insurance is probably great. With the limited income that most individuals have at this stage of their lives, it is generally possible to buy an adequate amount of insurance only if a term policy is selected. Whole life policies are so much more expensive than term that insufficient insurance will be purchased if whole life is chosen.

The disadvantage of rising premiums with term insurance should be considered, but a person's need for insurance may well decline as he grows older, so the amount of insurance carried can be reduced. Remember that choosing term means that you will have to set aside a savings fund on your own. Also, when you talk to a life insurance agent take into account that his commission on a whole life policy will be considerably larger than on a term policy of the same size.

50. Check Consumer Reports
Before Buying a Life Insurance Policy

One of a conscientious shopper's more difficult tasks is to compare life insurance policies on the basis of cost. Life insurance provisions vary so much from one policy to another that premium size alone is not an accurate guide. Policies accumulate savings at different rates and have special clauses, for example. Thus, a $10,000 policy sold by one company might actually be a better buy than a similar policy sold by another firm even though the former requires higher premium payments.

In an effort to make policies more easily comparable, the insurance industry has developed an index to measure something called the *interest-adjusted cost*. This is an attempt to take into account the time value of the money a person invests in a policy. Companies often include this index in their policies, and comparative figures for various policies sold by different companies may generally be obtained from your state insurance commission. If you have nothing else to go by, at least ask a salesman for the index for the policy that is being presented and take time to compare it to the indices of similar policies sold by other firms.

Unfortunately, even the index of interest-adjusted cost is not an ideal measure of cost among policies. For one thing, it is possible for companies to manipulate a policy's provisions in order to improve the policy's index. For another, the index does not provide a measure for the value of some policy features such as loan availability and the privilege of converting to another type of policy.

If premium size is a bad guide and the interest-adjusted cost index, although an improvement, may be misleading, what can a person do? The best advice is to seek independent guidance, and the best guidance may well be the periodic studies on life insurance undertaken by Consumers Union. This nonprofit consumers' organization investigates the features of various policies sold by a large number of companies and ranks them according to cost. Policies are differentiated according to size, type, and age of the insured, so it is possible to obtain a fairly accurate representation of cost comparisons among different policies in which you are interested. As of this writing, the most recent figures are available in the February (term insurance) and March (ordinary insurance) 1980 issues of *Consumer Reports*. These may be found in most libraries. Before you buy a life insurance policy at least take the trouble to investigate how the policy you are being sold compares. If it does not compare favorably, you should probably talk to another agent.

51. Do Not Purchase Life Insurance on the Lives of Your Children

Insurance agents often find new parents easy prey for the sale of life insurance contracts on their child, with the parents listed as the beneficiaries. A number of justifications are cited for making the sale, and although most of them are fallacious, parents are many times so anxious to provide their children with some type of security (no matter what it costs) that they are unlikely to worry about making a reasoned decision.

One of the arguments used in favor of purchasing insurance on a child is that proceeds from the policy can be used to offset burial expenses in the event the child dies. While these expenses may put some financial strain on a number of families, the purchase of an insurance policy would be a relatively expensive method of meeting this need. Another argument is that it is much less expensive to purchase insurance at a young age. While it is true that the premiums are lower, the purchase of something that is of questionable value cannot very well be described as less expensive. On the contrary, buying a product that is not needed is quite expensive regardless of the price. Some of the arguments are concerned with the savings portion of life insurance. For example, it may be stressed that taking out a policy at an early age will teach a child the virtues of thrift or that savings which build up over the years can be used to pay for a college education. Since many experts question whether life insurance is a good method of saving, there are almost surely better ways available to accomplish these goals. In any case, if this is the real reason for buying a policy, the portion of each premium that actually goes for protection would be wasted. Perhaps the one valid argument for buying a policy on a child is that you will be protecting against the possibility that the child will not be insurable (bad health, for example) when the time comes that insurance is normally purchased. While this is a real risk, purchasing a policy on a young child is a very expensive remedy.

If you think the reason to purchase life insurance is to protect against financial loss, then buying a policy on a child is of very questionable value. In fact, if extra insurance is needed, it is more likely that it is needed on the life of the breadwinner, not a child. If you are a parent, you will probably do your child a bigger favor by taking out additional insurance on your own life rather than by buying a policy on your child's life. If you feel you have enough insurance and want to start a savings plan for your child, consider some of the many alternatives to life insurance.

52. Think Twice about Buying Travel Insurance

If you are afraid to fly and feel unlucky, what is the best way of making sure that you arrive safe and sound at your destination? You simply bet against yourself and buy a little extra life insurance before you board the airplane. After all, if you are as unlucky as you think you are, there is no way the plane can crash if you are heavily insured.

As silly as this reaction may seem, the life insurance industry makes millions of dollars off people with this type of fear. The sales booths and insurance machines found at nearly every airport in the country are monuments to the fear and to the companies that profit because of it. For individuals that travel more often, insurance companies sell a common carrier accident policy that will pay death benefits if the insured dies because of an accident on a common carrier (e.g., scheduled airline, train, or bus service) anytime during the year. The policy you purchase at the airport generally covers that trip only.

So what is wrong with purchasing these policies? Two things, really. First of all, they are quite expensive on the basis of the benefits the company expects to pay. It is quite expensive to sell relatively small policies with short maturities and low premiums, and these high expenses are passed on to you. Even though the premiums may seem low, the remote possibility of a benefit payment makes these policies a bad buy. Remember, the policies generally pay benefits only in the event of death or injury due to travel on a common carrier.

The fact that you thought it necessary to purchase this insurance may indicate that you feel you are underinsured. If this is the case, a wiser choice would be to forego travel insurance and use the money to increase your basic life insurance coverage. After all, statistics clearly show that a person is more likely to die from something other than a travel-related accident. If you feel you already have a sufficient amount of life insurance, then the purchase of travel insurance is unnecessary.

53. Do Not Purchase Multiple Health Insurance Policies

In spite of what you may think, it is usually not possible to receive benefits in excess of medical expenses even though two or more health insurance policies are owned. You may feel that this is unfair since you have been paying premiums to two separate companies. Unfortunately, it is not only your feelings that will be hurt, but your pocketbook as well. Multiple health insurance policies are not a wise use of insurance dollars.

So what happens if you do have more than one policy? In the event of a claim, one policy will be classified as the primary policy and payment will be made according to the terms of that policy. An additional policy may pay the difference between your actual expenses and the amount that is paid by the primary policy (if the primary policy does not pay the entire bill), but it will generally not pay the same amount over again. The reason, of course, is that it would pay you to become sick and run up large medical bills if you could collect more than once on the same expense. Why not stay in the hospital a couple of extra days and make some easy money?

To clear up a confusing concept, let us use a specific example. Suppose you have two policies and each is $100 deductible (you pay the first $100) with an 80% coinsurance clause (the insurance company pays 80% of your expenses above $100). Both of these features are fairly standard in a health insurance policy. Now assume you run up $2,500 in medical expenses. The primary insurer will pay 80% of the expenses above $100, or $1,920. Of the remaining $580, the second policy may pay $464 (80% of $580), $384 (80% of the difference between $580 and the $100 deductible), or all $580 (80% of expenses above $100 with a maximum of what is not paid by the primary insurer). The amount paid by the secondary insurer depends upon the exact terms of the contract. However, it would be quite unusual to collect benefits in excess of total expenses.

When you are concerned about having sufficient medical insurance to help pay the bills in the event of a serious accident or illness, you should concentrate premium dollars on providing one good policy. If you currently have two or more policies in force, you could improve the coverage by devoting the extra premiums to improving benefits (e.g., increasing maximum coverage) on your basic policy.

54. Include Long Waiting Periods in Disability Insurance Policies

Disability insurance is designed to provide you with an income if you temporarily or permanently lose your ability to earn a livelihood due to a serious illness or accident. Assuming you are not independently wealthy and that you must rely on earnings from your job to meet everyday living expenses, there is little doubt that you need some form of disability income insurance. In fact, it is quite likely that this type of coverage is more important than life insurance for most individuals.

The cost of a disability policy depends upon a number of factors, including a person's occupation and age, the size of the payments that will be made, the definition of disability, the maximum number of payments that will be paid, and the waiting period between when disability occurs and the time the first payment is to be made. Your problem in buying this type of insurance is deciding which of these items to compromise on so you can obtain the best policy for the money.

Remember that the purpose of insurance is to transfer the risk of possible financial losses that you do not feel you can assume yourself. In the case of losing your income due to sickness or injury, it is a long-term disability that is most damaging. As a result, it is generally best to accept a relatively long waiting period (sometimes called an elimination period), say three to six months, and apply the savings toward extending the maximum period of time over which payments will be made. For example, many disability policies stop all payments after one or two years. If you are still disabled at the end of the payment period, it is your problem. And quite a problem it is.

The length of the waiting period you can accept will be influenced by such things as the amount of savings you have available to live off immediately following a disability, the size of income that will not be affected (income of spouse, interest and dividend income, etc.), and obligations that must be met (mortgage payments, food bills, etc.). Only you can decide the length of time you can get along once your earnings are cut off. Also keep in mind that many employers will continue to pay an employee's salary for a period of time after a disability occurs.

And how much can you save by accepting a longer waiting period? For a 35-year-old male in the best occupational classification (e.g., teacher), one large insurance company charges (per $100 a month in benefits) $32.20 per year for a policy with a 30-day waiting period and benefits payable until age 65. If the waiting period is extended to 180 days, the cost drops to $21.50. Thus, this individual could cut his premium by about one-third by extending the waiting period from 30 days to 180 days.

55. Do Not Buy Personal Property Insurance on Property You Would Not Replace

The purchase of insurance is a transferring of the risk of financial loss to someone else (the insurance company). It is most useful, then, when you do not feel you are able to absorb the potential loss yourself. For example, most homeowners would not be able to absorb the financial consequences of the loss of their home because of a fire or windstorm, so they transfer this risk by purchasing a homeowner's insurance policy. Likewise, individuals cannot ordinarily afford to replace the contents of their home, so they make sure they are also covered for losses to the personal property within their house.

Most homeowner's policies automatically include coverage for personal property contents—generally to an amount equal to 40 or 50% of coverage carried on the structure. For example, if your house is covered to a maximum of $50,000, the same policy will probably cover the contents for a loss of up to $20,000 or $25,000. Since different types of homeowner's policies are available, individuals should check with their insurance agents to make sure exactly what is covered in their policies.

Most of these policies do not provide full coverage for very valuable items you may own. For example, stamp and coin collections, jewelry, furs, and silverware must generally be insured separately through a personal articles floater policy. This policy will specify the articles, their value, and the types of losses that are insured. The more articles you include and the greater their value, the more a personal articles floater policy will cost.

Suppose you have some valuable property that would fall in these categories. Should you insure them or should you take your chances? An important factor in making your decision is first deciding if the articles would be replaced in case of loss. For example, you may have inherited some jewelry and an expensive silverware set from your parents. If these are important to you primarily as nostalgic keepsakes rather than as investments or useful articles, you probably would not replace them if they were stolen or damaged in a fire. It is questionable whether you should carry extra insurance on these items. Insurance should be looked upon as a cost to be minimized, because on an overall basis it is a losing proposition. Before you include a specific article on a personal articles floater policy ask yourself if you would replace the article if it were lost. If the answer is no, think twice about the insurance.

56. Consider Canceling Collision Insurance on an Older Car

Automobile collision coverage is designed to cover damage to the insured's car, regardless of who is at fault, in the event of a collision with another object (usually another car) or if the insured's car upsets. For example, if you run into another automobile, or a telephone pole, or if your car turns over on a slick road, it is your collision coverage that will pay for repairs. Damage you cause to someone else's car is covered by your property damage insurance, and damage to your car that is caused by someone else's car is covered by the other's property damage insurance. If the other driver has no insurance, your collision policy will cover your damages, although your insurance company has the right to sue the other driver.

Collision insurance is written so as to pay for the repairs to your car—or to reimburse you for the market value of the car in the event the cost of repairs exceeds the value of the car. If you run a $500 automobile into your garage door and the repair estimate is $900, the maximum you can recover is $500. In fact, you will probably recover less than this since most collision policies contain a $100 or $200 deductible feature, making you pay for the first $100 or $200 of damages.

It is necessary for most individuals to carry collision coverage on a new car (you will have no choice if you are financing it) because the value of the car represents such a significant portion of their assets that they cannot afford the possibility of so large a loss. However, as a car grows older and its value declines, the value of collision coverage becomes much more questionable. The idea in purchasing insurance is to transfer the possibility of losses you cannot handle yourself. Remember that overall, insurance is a losing proposition and should only be used when necessary. Paying insurance premiums to transfer potential losses of $700 or $800 may well be a bad buy.

In deciding whether to cancel collision insurance, find out what the coverage is costing and how much you would recover in the event your car were demolished. Do not forget to consider the deductible amount that you will not recover, and also remember that a casualty loss in excess of $100 that is not recovered through insurance is allowed as an itemized deduction on your income taxes. Thus, if you itemize and are in the 35% marginal tax bracket, a $500 casualty loss would result in tax savings of $140, so that the actual cost is only $360. You must also decide if you have the financial resources to absorb such a loss.

chapter eight

Stretching
food dollars

57. Eat at Home

Has anybody ever told you that food prices are so high in the super-markets that it is less expensive to eat out than it is to eat at home? Well don't you believe it. If food costs are high in the supermarkets, they are even higher in the restaurants. Restaurant owners cannot make money by selling you prepared meals for less than the food alone would cost in the grocery store. In fact, a rule of thumb used in the restaurant business is that if food costs amount to more than 35% of the price charged for meals, it is unlikely the restaurant will be profitable. Even if the restaurant operator can buy food more cheaply than you, he cannot buy it this much cheaper.

If it is so much more expensive to eat out, why have Americans spent increasingly larger portions of their food dollars at restaurants? Who knows. Maybe it is because it is more convenient, because it saves time, or because an increasing number of people actually believe it is less expensive to eat out. Of course, an increasing number of Americans are also going over their heads into debt, so just because other people do something does not mean it is necessarily best for you.

This is not meant to convince you that you should never eat a meal out. It is, however, designed to keep you from rationalizing that it is cheaper to do so. Even the time you are supposed to save is a myth. How long have you waited at a restaurant table to get a pizza? And how long did it take (and how much did it cost) to drive to the restaurant in the first place?

The secret to eating at home more often is to make it less of an effort and more of an enjoyment. One big help is a microwave oven. Even if it costs you $300, $400, or $500, you will find that it will pay for itself in short order if it keeps you at home. And the time saved in meal preparation will amaze you.

Another secret is to have an understanding of how to purchase groceries and what foods are good for you. For a good (and free) 28-page booklet write the Office of Governmental and Public Affairs, U.S. Department of Agriculture, Washington, D.C. 20250 and ask for *Your Money's Worth in Foods*. The booklet also contains a list of other free publications from the Department of Agriculture on buying, storing, and preparing foods.

58. Adjust Your Menu to the Good Buys

Are you the type of person that decides what you want to eat and then looks for the best place to buy the food? Worse yet, do you simply go out and buy what you want at the most convenient store? Although the first method of shopping is clearly superior to the second, there is still a much better way to organize your food purchases: build your menus around seasonal specials and sale items.

One of the easiest methods of saving on food dollars is to adjust your purchases to what is a "good buy." For example, since the supply of cattle for slaughter is much less flexible than the supply of hogs and, even more so, the supply of poultry, beef prices often go through extremely wide swings. During some periods beef is much more costly than pork or poultry, while in others it is very competitive. When beef is relatively plentiful, you should take advantage of the opportunity to include it in your diet. At other times you should avoid it by utilizing pork or chicken, depending upon which is cheaper.

The same type of reasoning applies to fresh fruits and vegetables. These items are seasonal in both supply and price, so it is possible to obtain some very good buys at certain times of the year. At other times, they will be quite scarce and carry high prices. When these foods are in abundance make it a point to schedule them on your menu.

Occasionally, you will find times when a flood, drought, freeze, or strike has created a shortage in a particular product. For example, suppose that extremely wet weather has slowed the harvest of lettuce in California. First, since a large amount of lettuce is already in the distribution pipeline, it should be possible to purchase some heads before the price rise hits the retail grocery stores. Stores generally set prices for a week at a time, and it will be at least a short period before the stores feel the full effect of rising costs. Once the high price hits and you have exhausted your own supply, you should begin substituting other vegetables for lettuce. Perhaps you would find making cabbage into slaw acceptable, for example.

Grocery stores will often feature certain products by charging lower-than-normal prices. A consumer should take account of these specials in menu planning. If one store is offering particularly good prices on dairy products, then meals should be planned around these items. If pasta products are the featured foods, for example, then meals could include spaghetti or macaroni.

The important lesson to be learned here is that you should remain sufficiently flexible in your eating habits to take advantage of bargains and avoid products in short supply. If you are too rigid, you may end up paying more than necessary.

59. Take Your Lunch to Work

One of the easiest methods of saving money on a consistent basis is to tote your lunch to work. The actual savings depend upon where you work and the types of eating establishments that are nearby. And if no restaurants are close, so that you would have to drive in order to find a place to eat, your savings from brown-bagging will be even greater. Assuming that lunch at a restaurant costs from $2.00 (fast food) to $4.00 (medium-price buffet), you should be able to save at least $7 to $15 per week by packing your own lunch.

The secret is to take lunches that offer variety and that are not too troublesome to fix. In other words, don't get into a position of where you dread to make your bag lunch or you dread to eat what you have made. Either instance will soon result in turning to restaurants ever more frequently until you are again eating out every day.

A major asset in brown-bagging is access to a refrigerator at your place of work. This allows a much wider variety of lunch possibilities, including items that are quite easy to fix but that need to be kept cool. For example, salads are low in calories and quite inexpensive to make. In addition, taking fruits and vegetables in place of cookies and potato chips is more nutritious.

Try to coerce some fellow workers in the joint purchase of a used refrigerator. You should be able to acquire one relatively inexpensively by checking the newspaper classifieds or self-service laundry bulletin boards. If you don't have any luck here, try to interest one other person into going together on the purchase of a new small refrigerator. Even if you have to buy one yourself (look for one on sale at a discount store), it should pay for itself in short order if you are saving $10 to $15 per week on lunch.

Another way to make taking your lunch more enjoyable is to have a microwave oven at work. Again, you may be able to convince your employer to provide one or you might talk to some fellow employees about joining together in a joint purchase. These appliances are particularly valuable at lunchtime when most people are in a hurry to eat. They make it easier to utilize leftovers from home and allow a person to have hot meals. Increased variety will decrease the temptation for you to duck out to a restaurant.

60. Get Organized before Shopping for Groceries

"Now, let's see, what is it I am supposed to buy in here?" "Don't I have a coupon for that somewhere?" "Where is it that bread is three loaves for a dollar?" If these sound like your murmurings as you wander through the supermarket, you are most surely spending more on groceries than you should. You need to get organized.

The key ingredient to intelligent grocery shopping is to get organized before you leave home. The first order of business is to make a list of the items you must have. This might include such staples as sugar, bread, milk, and salt. Next, list the things you would like to buy this week but could postpone for a week or so without suffering too much. This list might consist of things like yogurt, pickles, pizza sauce, bacon, and apples.

The second part of your organization plan should consist of scouring supermarket advertisements in the newspapers and finding the stores that are offering the best price on the items you need. If there do not appear to be any special prices on the discretionary items on your list, postpone buying them until next week when they may go on sale. You should also use the newspaper advertisements to make note of what articles are being run on special this week so that you can add these to your list. For example, if a store is running a good sale on tomato soup, tuna fish, or some other items you do not currently need but can store, you should include these. Also, if a store is offering an especially good sale on a more perishable food such as lettuce, pork chops, or oranges, you may want to substitute this for some other thing you had planned to buy. Always remember to plan your menu around sale items.

Once you have the lists completed, it is time to browse through your coupon book for cents-off coupons on the items you plan to buy. Pull the coupons out and clip them together by store. It is also important to keep track of especially good coupons such as those for free merchandise or large amounts off, so that they will not expire unused. Be sure to take the coupon book with you when you go shopping in case you have overlooked something or you run into some unadvertised specials.

When you decide upon the shopping route to take, plan an efficient one so as not to waste time and gasoline. Try to eliminate stores from your list if you are able to buy the same merchandise at a similar price at another store you plan to visit. If two or more stores offer the same price on an item, you may as well buy at a store that gives stamps. Unless the item involves a large expenditure, however, it is unlikely you would want to make a special trip just to get some stamps. You should also use coupons for free merchandise at these stores since price is unimportant. Most of all, stick to your list. Supermarkets are laid out to persuade you to purchase things you might not otherwise buy. Keep this in mind when you see those nice shining apples that are selling at 79 cents per pound.

61. Limit Supermarket Purchases to Groceries

Believe it or not, supermarkets typically earn relatively low profit margins on their sales. They try to make up for this by increasing the volume of sales produced by a store. The idea is that even if they don't make much by selling a box of cereal, if they can sell enough boxes, their total profits will be respectable. The profitability of selling groceries has been reduced to such a low return because of the very competitive nature of the supermarket business. Store managers know that the way to draw customers is to keep grocery prices low.

In an attempt to improve their profitability, supermarkets have continued to add more and more nongrocery items to their shelves. Records, magazines, paperback books, kitchen utensils, paper towels, toothpaste, soaps—the list goes on and grows larger by the year. The hope is that shoppers will purchase these items when they make their weekly trip to the supermarket. After all, if a person needs toothpaste, it is more convenient to pick it up while in the supermarket than it is to make a special trip to a discount store.

The drawback to this convenience is that nonfood products are generally more expensive at a supermarket than at a discount store. If the supermarket business is so competitive, how can they get away with charging high prices on items like health and beauty aids? People generally patronize a supermarket because of low grocery prices, not low toothpaste prices. Supermarkets run specials on grocery items in the hope that you will buy other grocery and nongrocery goods at regular prices.

And where should you buy these nongrocery items that are usually overpriced in the supermarket? Just ask yourself what types of stores often advertise these goods at low prices in order to attract shoppers. The answer is discount variety stores and drugstores that try to make their profits on something else such as appliances and prescriptions. Limit your supermarket purchases to grocery items. Buy the brooms and soap somewhere else.

62. Understand How Supermarkets Are Laid Out to Try to Trap You

Nearly all stores display merchandise in such a way as to entice consumers to spend more money. In fact, for most retailers, layout is just another form of advertising. This is true for clothing stores, hardware stores, discount stores, and supermarkets. There is nothing illegal or particularly wrong with this since in many cases it simply amounts to locating merchandise so that it is easy to find. In some instances, however, the intent is to encourage shoppers to buy products they would ordinarily pass up or to tempt them into substituting an item that is more profitable to the seller. Nowhere is this art practiced with more finesse than at the supermarket.

Supermarkets are generally laid out in such a way as to get customers to (1) spend more time in the store; (2) become exposed to as many items as possible; (3) pay more attention to the most profitable items; and (4) buy impulsively. Once a consumer understands some of the marketing gimmicks that are used in an attempt to accomplish these goals, it is easier to keep to the task at hand—getting the most value for your money.

One of the major ploys used by most supermarkets is to place low-priced impulse items such as cigarettes, candy, magazines, and other inexpensive merchandise next to the checkout lanes. The idea, of course, is that while you are waiting to be checked through you will thumb through a magazine and choose to buy it or decide to purchase a candy bar. In most cases, these impulse items are either things you could buy more cheaply elsewhere or items you normally would not buy at all.

Another favorite trick is to place the items the store manager wants you to buy at eye level on the shelves. Thus, when you reach for the pickles, peanut butter, catsup, and pizza mix you plan to buy, you are more likely to buy the brand and size the store wishes you to buy. Since the best deal for the store may be the worst deal for you, do not be in a hurry so that you can take time to compare brand, size, and price.

Many supermarkets will place sale items throughout the store so that it is necessary for a shopper to pass by forty products he was not planning to buy in order to find the one or two in which he is interested. By leading a shopper on such a hunt, the store manager expects the consumer to purchase some extra items. Some supermarkets will accomplish much the same result by placing often-used items such as bread and milk at the back of the store. The trick here is to buy what you came for and ignore everything else.

Other supermarket tricks include placing produce near the store entrance to slow down your shopping spree (even though, by the time you check out, the bananas will be smashed), having wide aisles in high-profit areas, and making special displays for items that are generally slow sellers.

63. Take a Calculator to the Supermarket

You know that atomic scientists, economics professors, corporate presidents, and store managers find calculators an indispensable part of performing their jobs. Do you know that a calculator is also one of the best investments a shopper can make? That's right, the little pocket calculator that you can slip in your purse or shirt pocket will save you many times its original cost in just a relatively short period of time. And you do not have to spend hours learning a lot of complicated financial theory. You merely need to know how to divide.

The next time you go to the supermarket make it a point to notice the various sizes in which a particular product is available. In many instances a large size might contain twice the content of the small size, while a jumbo container, in turn, contains twice as much as the large size. Such a system makes it easy for a shopper to calculate the cost relative to the quantity that is being purchased. For example, tomato paste is generally available in both 6- and 12-ounce cans. Thus, you know immediately that if the 12-ounce can costs less than twice as much as the 6-ounce can, the larger size offers the better price (if you need that much). No problem here. Unfortunately, not all products are sold in such sensible sizes. If you don't believe it, just trot on down to the shelves that are stacked full of peanut butter jars. Peanut butter is nearly always sold in 18-, 28-, and 40-ounce jars, which makes it extremely difficult to compare value among the different sizes. If only they would pack them in 18-, 27-, and 36-ounce jars. Or 15-, 30-, and 45-ounce jars. But don't hold your breath waiting for such a change. Now go to the laundry products section and take a glance at the boxes of detergent. You will nearly always find a giant-size box containing 49 ounces (beware of "giant" boxes that only contain 42 ounces), while the next larger size is an 84-ounce box. Now look at the hand soap, which is usually packaged in 3½-, 5-, and 7-ounce bars. If you really want some confusion, try the cereals.

Why are products packaged in such odd sizes? Do you suppose the manufacturers are trying to pull the wool over our eyes? One way to fight back is to limit your shopping to stores that display unit prices. Thus, the store will show both the cost per can or box and also the cost per ounce or pound. An increasing number of stores are using unit pricing as a way to provide consumers with more information. However, even here you may run into difficulty. When items are temporarily put on sale, shelf prices are often left unchanged. As a result, you may have trouble determining relative values on the very items in which you are most interested.

Another way to defend yourself is to take a pocket calculator with you when you go shopping. This way, the next time you are in the soap section and unsure which size box to buy, you merely need to whip out the electronic marvel, punch a couple of buttons, and presto—the price per ounce is displayed right before your eyes. The best calculators to use are the small, thin models that can easily be slipped into your pocket. Watch for sales and you will probably find one for about $10. Make it a habit to take your calculator with you whenever you go shopping. You never know when you might run into a bargain and not even know it.

64. Use Powdered Milk

Even though fresh milk is often used as a promotional item by grocery and convenience stores to draw customer traffic, it can still be relatively expensive. One of the reasons for the steep price is a government agricultural policy that encourages it. Except for writing letters of protest to government officials, however, there is not much a single consumer can do about this. There is a way to cut down on the cost of milk, though. Substitute nonfat dry ("powdered") milk for fresh milk.

Nonfat dry milk can often be purchased for about half the cost of fresh milk. Your savings depend upon the amount of milk you use and the size container you normally buy. Both fresh and dry milk are less expensive per quart the larger the container you purchase. One of the great advantages of dry milk is that, since you can store it for relatively long periods, it is possible to buy a large package and obtain a lower per-unit cost even though you are not a big consumer of milk. On the other hand, small users must generally buy fresh milk by the quart or take the chance of spoilage. Large consumers of milk should compare the price of fresh milk by the gallon with dry milk to get a valid cost comparison.

And how do these two products compare in terms of nutrition? Except for vitamins A and D, which are removed with the fat and water during processing, nonfat dry milk contains all the nutrients of fluid whole milk. These vitamins are generally added back to the mixture to make fortified nonfat dry milk so that the end product is essentially the same from a nutritional standpoint. In terms of calories, nonfat dry milk contains the same as fresh skim milk (about 90 calories per 8 fluid ounces), but significantly less than milk with 2% milk-fat (130 calories) and whole milk (160 calories).

If you have become accustomed to the richness of whole milk, you might try to wean yourself to the dry version by mixing the two. Begin with mostly whole milk and gradually increase the percentage of dry milk until you find a mix with which you are comfortable. Even if you find you cannot drink nonfat dry milk as a beverage, you should find it relatively painless to substitute for whole milk in cooking. If your only use of milk is in cooking, you should be able to avoid whole milk altogether and save calories as well as money.

65. Understand the Economics of Egg Buying

You go to the grocery with a simple task—buy some eggs for tomorrow's breakfast. As you round the aisle and face the dairy section you also face one of a shopper's greatest dilemmas: should you buy the small eggs in the pink cartons, the medium eggs in the blue cartons, the large eggs in the white cartons, or the extra large variety in the yellow cartons? To make the confusion even greater, some stores also carry jumbo and peewee sizes. Once you learn some basics of eggs, the decision will not seem so difficult.

Egg grades of AA, A, and B refer to the interior quality and shell appearance. The grades mainly concern appearance with grades AA and A recommended for frying and poaching and less expensive grade B for general cooking and baking. Shell color is determined by hen breed and does not affect the flavor, nutrition, cooking performance, or grade of the egg.

Eggs are sized according to a minimum weight requirement per dozen. These are: jumbo (30 ounces), extra large (27 ounces), large (24 ounces), medium (21 ounces), small (18 ounces), and peewee (15 ounces). The size differences must be used in conjunction with price in deciding upon the most economical buy. As a general rule, you should buy the next larger size if it does not cost 13% more than the size below it. For example, if a dozen large eggs sell for ninety cents, while mediums cost 82 cents, you should buy the large size since there is less than a 13% difference in price between the two. For a general guideline in finding the best buy for your money, use the following:

When the price of a dozen large eggs is:	41-48¢	49-56¢	57-64¢	65-72¢	73-80¢	81-88¢	89-96¢
Buy the larger size if the price difference between it and the next larger size is:	6¢	7¢	8¢	9¢	10¢	11¢	12¢

chapter nine

Stretching household dollars

66. Buy a Snug House

"We really didn't need nearly this much space but decided to buy the house anyway because it is always better to have too much room than too little." The person that last told you this is probably over his or her head in debt and still driving an automobile that gets 8 miles to the gallon. The old axiom that "bigger is better" is falling by the wayside for houses as well as for automobiles. Perhaps a better rule would now be "buy only as big as you absolutely require."

Big homes are much like big cars in that they cost more to buy, cost more to run, and may well end up to be much more difficult to sell. In spite of this, some people continue to buy houses that have extra bedrooms (in case a family of six comes to visit), a separate dining room (used twice a year), and separate living and family rooms (one of which is never used). All of this additional space results in extra expenses.

First, large houses cost more to construct because they consume more labor and materials and may require a larger and more expensive lot. Because the home costs more, the owner of a large house will have higher property taxes to pay and a more expensive homeowner's insurance policy to buy. Of course, these two expenses will persist as long as the person continues to own the home. In addition, a house with more and bigger rooms requires more furniture to fill it. Operating costs will also be greater for a larger home. It will cost more to heat and cool, and maintenance expenses will be higher. There is more carpet to replace, more wood and trim to paint, and more shingles to fix. And even if you try to construct an energy-efficient home, you will have to buy more insulation and additional double-pane windows in order to do the job.

Since people are becoming more conscious about the operating costs of a house, being able to show reasonable utility and maintenance expenses is becoming increasingly crucial in selling a home. As utility prices, taxes, and labor costs continue to rise there is little reason to expect this trend to be reversed. If you have extra money to put into a home, put it into a better location, a nicer lot, or additional energy-saving features that can be justified on an economic basis.

67. Consider Spraying for Pests Yourself

You say you have seen roaches using your kitchen counter as a parade ground? Or maybe you just bought a new house and are concerned about termites? You should call an exterminating company, have it spray for the pests, and then sign a contract with the exterminator to make sure the bugs do not return. Or should you?

Depending upon the area of the country in which you live, different insects will be of concern. In the Southeast, for example, termites are a major problem because they can cause so much damage. In other areas, the insects may be more of a bother to the senses than a threat to do physical damage. Whether they cause actual damage or not, most people do not like to have them around.

Many individuals handle pest problems by contracting with an exterminating company. For a monthly or annual fee, the company will make periodic inspections and spray for pests. In addition, if insects are encountered between inspections, you generally may call the exterminator and have the problem taken care of at no additional charge. The fee for contracting with an exterminating company will vary with the type of service performed and the extent of a firm's guarantee. In many cases, a contract will guarantee only that the pests will be eliminated and not specify that the exterminator will be responsible for damages caused by the insects. This differentiation is especially important in areas where termites are prevalent.

If you are currently paying an exterminator to keep your home free of insects, you may be able to save some money by doing the same job yourself. The nice thing about this is that the only equipment you need is a $20 sprayer that is available at nearly any discount store or garden supply house. And how do you know when to spray, what chemicals to use, or even what insects cause problems in the area where you live? It is easy. Simply call your local county extension agent and ask these very questions. Most are quite familiar with the topic and will be glad to help. The agent will probably even be able to supply you with publications on the more common types of pests in your area.

If you decide to take on the job yourself, be sure to call a number of stores about chemical prices. The costs of pesticides can vary a great deal depending upon container size, brand, and retailer.

68. Buy Your Own Telephone

It is now possible for individuals to purchase their own telephones and connect into the local telephone service. In fact, the telephone companies themselves are among the biggest promoters of customers owning their own phones. However, you should be warned that it is illegal to plug in your phone without first telling the phone company that you are planning to do so. And you still have to pay the phone company a monthly fee since you will be utilizing its lines, switching equipment, operators, etc. In fact, about the only thing different is that you will now own your phone instead of leasing it from the telephone company. Plus you will be saving some money—maybe.

Since the phone company does not have to provide you with a telephone, it will lower your monthly bill slightly. Although this savings varies from company to company and depends upon the type of phone you are replacing, at a minimum you should have your monthly fee cut by about 60 cents for each phone that you provide. Thus, you should save at least 60 cents X 12, or $7.20 per year on your telephone bills for each phone you replace. Whether this is a good deal or not depends upon how much you pay for a phone. If you are careful and look for sales, you should be able to find a plain white or beige one for close to $25 (check sales at Radio Shack, discount stores, and large retailers such as

Sears or Penney). In this case, monthly savings should repay the cost of the phone in a little over three years, so that your annual return will be about 30%, tax-free. Although a proper financial evaluation would also have to consider depreciation on the telephone (i.e., its wear and tear), the return is still quite high.

The potential savings for fancier models may well be even larger. For example, on one model that has a rotary dial on the handle, one telephone company charges a one-time fee of $5.81 plus an extra $1.45 per month. A similar phone can be purchased in a discount store for under $45. If you currently have this phone in your home and replace it with one that you purchase, you will be out an immediate $45. However, you will begin saving $2.05 per month ($1.45 extra charge for fancy phone plus 60 cents basic reduction) which amounts to $24.60 in the first year alone. Thus, if you replace the telephone company's fancy model with your own fancy model, your $45 investment will be recovered in less than two years.

The disadvantage of owning your own phone is that you are responsible for its maintenance. If it breaks, you must either pay to get it fixed or buy another one. If you report a problem to the phone company and the repairperson finds that the problem is actually with your phone and not the company's system, you will be charged for a service call (without getting your phone fixed). However, with the general reliability of phones these days, this seems like a pretty good gamble on your part. A good compromise is to lease one phone from the telephone company and purchase the phones that are used for extensions.

When you decide to buy your own phone be sure to shop carefully. Although the telephone companies sell a wide variety of phones, they often specialize in those that are in the medium to high end of the price range. If you only want a basic telephone, you can probably find a better deal somewhere else.

69. Consider a Party Line for Your Telephone

Although you might not know it, you can still have party line telephone service. And you ask, "Why would anyone want to be on a party line?" The answer, of course, is that you can save money, since a party line is less expensive than a private line. It does not cost the telephone company as much to provide customers with party line service, and this saving is passed on in the form of lower rates to customers who choose this service.

Many people think of party line service in terms of the telephone service that was provided years ago. That is, they remember when so many people were on the same line that it was difficult to make or receive a call because the line was always tied up. In addition, so many people on your line would be listening to your conversation that it would often be difficult to hear what was being said. It is unlikely you would be able to obtain this type of party line service today even if you desired it.

Most party line service is now of the two- or four-party variety, and some service areas only offer the former. As a result, it is generally only necessary to compete with one other family for the phone line. In some cases, it seems that no party ever ends up on the other part of a two-party line, so you actually have a private line for the price of a two-party line. Generally, however, there will be some mysterious person out there.

And how much will you save? The answer depends upon where you live and what you normally pay for private service. In general, a two-party line should reduce your basic monthly fee by 15 to 20%. Remember that this savings does not apply to extra charges such as those for Touch-Tone service or extensions. As a result, unless you have the most basic service, your savings will be less than 15 or 20% of your total bill. In dollar terms, you should save $2.00 or more per month by having two-party service.

As you can imagine, a party line is not without its drawbacks, especially if you are paired with someone that likes to spend a lot of time on the telephone. A major factor in your decision should rest with your lifestyle. If you work most of the day and spend a lot of weekends away from home, the inconvenience of a party line may be minimal because you do not use the phone much. On the other hand, if you or another family member are home a lot, the savings may not be worth the trouble. You should be aware that there is generally no charge to have a party line changed to a private line (or vice versa) in case you come to the conclusion you have made a mistake and want to make a change.

70. Investigate Putting Your Phone on Vacation Rate

You have decided to take the summer off and travel around the country in your new Volkswagen camper. Or perhaps you are planning to beat the winter snows of Rushville, Indiana and spend three months in Florida this year. Do you know that it is sometimes possible to save a few dollars by having your telephone put on suspended service or vacation rate? (Different companies use different names.)

Most telephone service areas allow their customers to place phones on an inactive status at a reduced rate. As a rule, your telephone service is temporarily disconnected at the company's central switchboard so that no incoming or outgoing calls may be placed through that number until service is resumed. You may generally instruct the telephone company to have a recorded message greet those who call your number during the time service is suspended. Something like "At the request of the customer, this number has temporarily been disconnected" is typical. Some companies will allow a message that refers callers to another number.

There may be a few conditions placed on suspended service, but they usually are not very restrictive. You must generally place your phone on the service for a minimum of one month, for example. Some phone companies also require you to have had regular service at that residence for at least one month. Others set a maximum amount of time you may place your phone on vacation rate. Customers in Indianapolis may not have the reduced rate for more than six consecutive months, for instance.

The amount of money you can save from this service, or whether you should even use it, depends upon a number of factors. For one, how long will you be away? The longer you plan to be gone, the more you will save. However, at some point it becomes cheaper to have service disconnected altogether. You can then pick up a phone and pay the regular reconnect fee when you return. Another major factor in your decision is the rate schedule of your telephone company, since fees vary widely from one part of the country to another. For example, in Valdosta, Georgia, using suspended service will cut your monthly charge in half, but you must pay an extra $10.40 to change it back to regular service. In Pittsburgh, there is an initial charge of $7 and your monthly fee will be reduced to a flat $1.32. In Phoenix, your monthly charge is reduced to half and there is no additional charge.

Before you leave on the trip, call the business office of your local phone company and get three pieces of information: (1) the basic monthly fee you are paying; (2) the cost of having service restored if you have it disconnected—this generally entails picking up a phone at a company store when you return; (3) the fee for having your service temporarily suspended. Figure the total cost of each alternative over the time you will be gone and choose the one that is cheapest. Keep in mind that if you have service disconnected (not suspended), you will probably be assigned a new telephone number when you return.

71. Buy a Nonmotorized Reel-Type Lawn Mower

Remember the old lawn mower your grandfather used to have? You know, the one that you had to push back and forth across the yard. Not only was it not self-propelled, it did not even have a motor to turn the blade. Well, those mowers are still available, but you have to look hard in order to find one. Modern America seems to have moved right past the old nonmotorized lawn mower and very few stores stock them anymore.

Nonmotorized lawn mowers offer a number of advantages over the new models. They are much more quiet so that you will preserve your own hearing in addition to offering your neighbors a little peace. They also provide you with additional exercise so that you can beautify your residence and your body at the same time. And although many newer motorized models have incorporated some basic safety features, they still cannot compete with the inherent safety of a nonmotorized mower. For those of you who are more concerned with a fine-looking yard than anything else, remember that reel-type mowers are used by professionals when jobs must really be done right.

All of these are good reasons to buy a nonmotorized reel-type mower. However, what we are concerned about here is saving money, and it is here that this piece of machinery stands head and shoulders above the competition. First, it costs less to buy. Good-quality reel mowers can be purchased new for anywhere between $50 and $80, which is about half what a medium-priced motorized mower costs. If you have a hard time finding one, look in a Sears or Penney catalog. Better yet, take in a few garage and yard sales. A second financial reason to own one of these mowers is that it costs nothing to operate. Perhaps a few drops of oil now and then, but that is about it. No high-priced gasoline to use and no running out of gas when you are half-done with the yard. Last, and perhaps best, nonmotorized reel-type mowers last a long, long time. Unlike motorized versions which are often hard to start and shake themselves to death in short order, nonmotorized mowers have almost nothing to go wrong.

There are limits to which you can take this suggestion. If you have an unusually large yard, it may be nearly impossible to rely solely on a nonmotorized mower. Likewise, even a medium-size yard may present difficulties for a working couple hoping to depend upon one of these mowers. However, for many individuals, owning a nonmotorized reel-type lawn mower is a good method of saving money. It will cost less to buy, cost less to run, and last longer. From a cost standpoint you really cannot ask for much more.

72. Examine the Economics of
Owning a Freezer before Purchasing One

As food prices continue to rise, and rise, and rise, and then rise some more, an increasing number of people are buying freezers as a way to keep from drowning in food bills. There is little doubt that freezers can lower food bills. However, it is important to consider the costs involved in owning a freezer, for it is possible that these may more than offset any direct savings on food.

There are four major costs of owning a freezer: depreciation, opportunity cost of the money invested, maintenance, and energy consumption. Depreciation cost stems from the fact that a freezer will eventually wear out and need to be replaced. If you assume an average life of fourteen years, yearly depreciation will be approximately 7% of the freezer's original price. The concept of opportunity cost is examined elsewhere in this book (see number 1). In the case of owning a freezer, it is the cost of having money invested in the freezer rather than using it somewhere else. For example, you could deposit the money in a savings account, invest it in common stock, or use it to help pay off the loan on your car. You should also include the opportunity cost of the money tied up in the food you have in the freezer. Even though freezers are relatively trouble-free, you can expect to have trouble every once in a while—especially when it gets some age on it. It would not seem unrealistic to assume you might need a service call every other year throughout its life. Energy cost will be determined both by energy consumption and by the cost of electricity where you live. Energy consumption, in turn, will depend primarily upon size and construction. Manufacturers must display estimated annual energy cost on all new models, so that this will be one of the easiest costs for you to determine.

To see how these costs may be estimated, suppose you are considering the purchase of a new freezer with 15 cubic feet of interior space. It is currently on sale for $400 and you think it will last about fourteen years. The annual cost of owning the freezer will be:

Depreciation	$ 28.60	(Original cost divided by expected life)
Opportunity cost:		(Assuming you could earn 10%)
$400 cost of freezer	40.00	
$200 contents	20.00	
Maintenance	20.00	(Estimated)
Electricity	70.00	(Information provided by manufacturer)
Annual cost	$178.60	

Now you must decide if you can save this much on food costs if you have a freezer. If you butcher your own hogs and grow your own vegetables, the answer is probably yes. If you are a city person who carefully shops supermarket specials, the savings may be much more questionable—especially if you are single or are married without children.

73. Think Twice about Appliance Service Contracts

When you buy a new appliance (or soon after purchasing a new home full of appliances) there will more than likely be an attempt to convince you to buy a service contract. Appliance service contracts are designed to cover both the labor and parts required to fix an appliance. Most consumers purchase the contracts to take effect when an appliance's regular warranty expires. Contracts are generally purchased on a yearly basis with the annual cost increasing as the appliance becomes older.

In a sense, a service contract is a form of insurance where the consumer is paying a yearly premium to transfer the cost of possible appliance repairs to someone else. The someone else, of course, is the appliance dealer or repair firm that sells the contract. In buying a service contract, a consumer is protecting himself against the possibility of incurring any repair expenses during a given time period.

The decision of whether or not to purchase a service contract should be made in exactly the same way as other insurance decisions. First, a person must have an idea of the types and monetary value of possible losses that may occur. These potential losses must then be compared with an individual's ability to pay for the repairs. For example, do you have the funds to pay for some major appliance repairs without becoming financially strapped? If not, you may end up borrowing money to pay the repair bills. Another important point that must be addressed is the use to which you put individual appliances. If you are single or married with no children, you probably eat out more often (use your range, dishwasher, microwave, and disposal less), dirty fewer clothes (use your washer and dryer less), and travel more (use your TV less) than if you are married with three or four small children. Since appliance repair contract costs are based upon average usage and average repair needs, a consumer who is a light user of an appliance would probably find that a service contract is over-priced and a bad buy. On the other hand, a large family might well find an appliance contract (especially on appliances such as a washer, dryer, and dishwasher) to be a good buy, since heavy usage can be expected to result in above-average repair needs.

In summary, if you are financially able to absorb repair costs, pur-chase an appliance service contract only if you can expect repair needs that are greater than average. One good method of judging frequency-of-repair needs is the use to which you put an appliance. The heavier the usage, the more likely a service contract on that appliance is a good buy. If you are not financially able to absorb repair costs, a service contract makes more sense even if you anticipate only average repair bills.

74. Shop for Prescription Drugs

When was the last time you saw prescription drug prices advertised in the newspaper? Or on the windows of the drug store? Or over the prescription counter at the drugstore? Depending upon where you have lived, there is a good chance that you have never seen prescription drug prices advertised in any of these places because such advertising is still prohibited in many areas. Under a ploy adopted by doctors, dentists, and lawyers, pharma-cists have argued that there is a great deal more to serving customers than simply filling orders. (This is sometimes true.) Price advertising would lead to cutthroat competition and actually not be in the best interest of the consumer, they argue, because it would damage the important personal relationship between pharmacists and their customers. In other words, professional ethics do not allow them to advertise.

While many individuals might question the connection between advertising and ethics, there is another relationship that appears to be more clear—advertising and prices. A lack of advertising means less con-sumer knowledge of prices and tends to result in market imperfections. In the prescription drug business this has produced large price differentials for the same drug from one store to another.

For you the market imperfection means that it is very important to shop carefully. One way to compare prices is to drive from store to store until you have located the one with the lowest price. A more sensible way is to use the telephone to call the druggists in your area and inquire about the price of filling a particular prescription. Be forewarned that some drugstores have a policy of not quoting on the phone their charge for filling a prescription. These stores might justify the practice on the basis that there is more to consider in filling a prescription than simply the price or that the pharmacist would spend too much of his or her time on the phone rather than in filling prescriptions. A less frequently cited reason, but one that may be more relevant, is that prices may be considerably higher than the prices that competitors are charging. Unless you have some overriding reason to act otherwise, you should generally avoid having prescriptions filled at drugstores that refuse to quote prices over the telephone.

There is no reason to go overboard on price shopping. If you have a relatively small one-time prescription, the money you would save by spending a half-hour on the phone and driving across town may not be worth the bother. On the other hand, if you are talking about a standing order (e.g., birth control pills), the savings could amount to a significant amount over a period of years. You may also find that for prescription drugs that lend themselves to standing orders, the price competition will be particularly intense because the stores like to have you coming in on a regular basis (hoping you will buy something else). Do not pass up the opportunity to take advantage of this competition.

75. Purchase Drugs by Their Generic Names

Believe it or not, it is often possible to buy what is essentially the same drug under various names at different prices. Consumers are probably most familiar with this practice when it comes to aspirin. *Aspirin* is the generic or "nonproprietary" name for a nonprescription painkiller that is sold under a variety of brand names such as St. Joseph's and Bayer. Whether you purchase a heavily advertised national brand at a small drugstore or a house brand at a drug chain or discount store you will be buying the same-quality product that must meet the same Food and Drug Administration (FDA) standards for that product.

Drug manufacturers that develop a new drug are permitted to patent their product for seventeen years. During that period, the manufacturer has the exclusive right to sell that product, which gives it time to build up a brand image among consumers. It may also license other companies to produce and sell the drug. Once the patent expires, the manufacturing and selling of the drug is opened up to other firms so long as they use the generic name or an alternative brand name. Regardless of whether a drug is sold under its generic name or a variety of brand names, it must meet the same FDA standards for safety, strength, purity, and effectiveness.

Examples of the same drug being sold under a variety of names abound. The widely used antibiotic tetracycline is sold under its generic name and under the better-known brand names of Tetracyn, Achromycin, and Sumycin. The drug ampicillin is available under 224 product labels even though it is produced by only 24 formulators. (Some companies put their brand names on drugs manufactured by other companies.)

Since the FDA has stated that it believes there is no significant difference in quality between generic and brand-name drugs, how is it that consumers end up buying a lot of high-priced drugs when they could purchase the equivalent product under its generic name for much less? Part of the reason is a lack of awareness that this practice actually takes place. Another is that some state laws forbid pharmacists to dispense any version of a drug product other than what has been specifically prescribed by the doctor. Since drug companies spend big dollars on promotional activities, it is quite likely a doctor will prescribe a drug by its brand name rather than its generic name.

What can you do? Ask your doctor to prescribe a drug by its generic name. In most cases he will. When you go to a pharmacy ask the druggist to fill the prescription with a generic version of the drug. If it is allowed in your state, he should be willing. If it is permitted and he will not abide by your request, go to another drugstore. To determine if this practice is permitted, call two or three pharmacies before having the prescription filled.

chapter ten

Stretching energy dollars

76. If You Plan to Insulate,
You Should Probably Start with the Attic

Everyone knows that the more heavily a home is insulated, the less heating and cooling it requires. However, most of us have only a limited amount of money to spend at any one time, so it is important that dollars be allocated where they can produce the greatest amount of savings.

As a general rule, insulation is most effective when added in the attic. During winter months heat tends to rise and escape through ceilings which have inadequate insulation, while during summer months the sun beats most directly on the roof causing heat to enter at this point. Because the roof usually represents the area of greatest heat loss during the winter and heat gain during the summer, it is often possible to obtain significant savings by adding insulation in this area.

The savings from adding insulation depends upon a number of factors. One, of course, is the cost involved. In this respect, the attic is at a relative advantage because it is generally easy to reach. In contrast, adding insulation to the walls of a house is a fairly complicated and expensive procedure. Another determinant of savings is the amount of insulation that your attic already contains, since additions of insulation bring diminishing returns. That is, you save significantly more from the first 6 inches of insulation than you do from adding 6 inches to an already existing 6 inches. Thus, installing insulation when 6 or more inches is already present may not produce enough savings to make the expense worthwhile. The total amount of insulation recommended by the Department of Energy is determined by the climate in which a house is located.

How much can a homeowner save by insulating the attic? One study estimates that energy consumption for heating and cooling will be cut by approximately 45% if 6 inches of insulation is installed in a ceiling that has no existing insulation. For a homeowner who normally spends $1,000 per year for heating and cooling, the $450 estimated savings will quickly return the cost of the improvement. In contrast, adding 6 inches to an already existing 6 inches will produce savings of only about 15% of energy costs.

For information applicable to your particular climate and home, call your local utility or county agent. They are generally glad to help, and in many cases each will be able to supply you with some informative publications. Two excellent government publications, *Making the Most of Your Energy Dollars* (70 cents) and *In the Bank or up the Chimney* ($1.70), are available from the Consumer Information Center, Pueblo, Colorado 81009. Free fact sheets on *How to Determine Your Insulation Needs, How to Install Insulation for Ceilings,* and *What to Look for in Selecting Insulation,* are available by writing Energy, U.S. Department of Agriculture, Washington, D.C. 20250.

77. Consider Energy-Efficient Appliances

Remember the days when appliances were purchased only on the basis of color, style, size, price, service, and manufacturer? Little thought was paid to how much electricity an appliance used, both because the cost was nominal and because information on electrical consumption was difficult to come by even if a buyer was interested. Well, those days have ended—at least for the smart consumer. Color, style, price, service, and manufacturer are still important considerations, of course. But the rising cost of electricity has made the energy efficiency of many appliances another important consideration. And now it is possible to compare energy consumption among models.

In 1975, Congress passed the Energy Policy and Conservation Act which requires the Federal Trade Commission to issue rules for disclosing energy cost information to consumers. Initial labeling commenced on major appliances manufactured after May 19, 1980, and applied to water heaters, room air conditioners, dishwashers, refrigerators, and washing machines. The disclosure was expanded to include furnaces and central air conditioners in 1981. The fairly large labels display the estimated energy cost for that particular model at the national average utility rate and compare it to the energy costs of other models of similar size and features. Although other models are not identified by brand name, it is easy to determine how a particular model stacks up against the competition. The label also shows the appliance's energy cost at various electric rates so you will want to know the cost of electricity where you live. To find it simply call your electric company. Remember that many electric companies charge on the basis of usage, so ask for the rate that applies to your particular residence.

Be forewarned that energy-efficient appliances nearly always cost more to purchase. However, you may be able to make up the higher cost in savings on your electric bill. It depends upon how heavily you use a given appliance and how much electricity costs in your particular area. For example, energy efficiency is much more important in New York City, where electric rates are quite high, than in Idaho or Washington State, where they are quite low. In general, if you can recover the higher initial cost of an energy-efficient appliance within ten years, you should probably choose it. To help in making your decision, ask the dealer for an Energyguide worksheet. You can also obtain one by writing the Department of Energy, Appliance Labeling Consumer Education, Washington, D.C. 20858.

78. Lower the Temperature on Your Water Heater

One of the surest, easiest, and least painful methods of reducing energy bills is to lower the temperature at which your hot water heater operates. In fact, in most uses you will not even be able to tell that the hot water is being heated to a lower temperature.

Energy consumption by a hot water heater will vary greatly among different households and depends on such factors as size of tank (a bigger tank has more surface area where heat is lost), water temperature inside the tank (a higher water temperature results in greater loss), temperature of the surrounding air (a lower surrounding temperature means more energy loss), a tank's insulating qualities (discussed in the next section), and, of course, the amount of hot water that is used. Despite these variations, a water heater is the second biggest energy user in most households (behind the heating-and-cooling unit). The Edison Electric Institute estimates that the average annual energy requirement for an electric water heater is 4,811 kilowatt-hours, or about 400 kilowatt-hours per month. At an average cost of 5 cents per kilowatt-hour, this would result in a cost of about $20 per month. (A kilowatt-hour, the standard measure of electrical usage, is the amount of electricity required to burn a 100-watt lightbulb for 10 hours.)

Most water heaters are set at a temperature of 140°F or above, even though a setting of 120°F should provide adequate hot water for most families. The exception to this is that some people recommend a water temperature of about 140°F for dishwashers in order to dissolve the dishwashing detergent (it still does not sanitize the dishes). The Department of Energy estimates you could save over 18% ($3.60 per month based on the figures above) if you reduced the temperature setting by 20 degrees or 6% if you reduced the setting by only 10 degrees. Of course, if your hot water heater is set at 150°F or higher, you can save additional money by reducing the temperature 30 or more degrees.

Somewhat surprisingly, most of the savings will not occur because of using water at a lower temperature, for in most uses you will simply increase the mix of hot water to cold water. For example, when running your bath water you will typically increase the proportion of hot water in order to obtain the same bath water temperature that you have always used. The majority of savings from a lower water heater temperature occurs because of the reduced loss of heat from the water pipes and from the water heater itself. When you run your shower, hot water is left in the pipes to cool when you are finished. The hotter the water left in the pipes, the more energy that has been consumed and wasted. Likewise for the hot water heater. The greater the temperature difference between the water inside the water heater and the outside temperature, the more heat that is lost to the surrounding air. Even if the water heater is inside, you will have heat escaping in the summer so that your air conditioner will have to work harder.

And how does a person go about lowering the temperature on the water heater? Get a screwdriver, turn off the electricity to the water heater (for safety's sake), and take off the small metal plate that is probably located at the bottom of the tank. A small screw can then be turned counterclockwise to lower the thermostat. If no temperature readings are available beside the screw, draw some water through the faucet near the bottom and test it with a thermometer.

79. Insulate Your Water Heater

A large part of the energy consumed by a water heater is actually wasted when heat is lost through the walls of the tank and the pipes that are in close proximity to the tank. The amount of energy lost in this manner depends upon a number of variables that were discussed in the last section. One of the factors mentioned, and an area where improvement is easiest to achieve, is the insulating quality of the water tank.

Most manufacturers of water heaters produce at least one super-insulated model, but these appliances are generally not well insulated. And since water heaters have relatively long lives, many of the units currently in use were designed and installed at a time when energy was much less expensive than it is today. Should you be building a new house or replacing an old tank, you would be well advised to purchase one of the efficient models. Likewise, as discussed in the previous section, you can save energy by reducing the temperature of the water in the tank.

One inexpensive method of reducing energy losses on your present unit is to purchase a layer of insulation to install around the tank and pipes. Insulation kits for this specific purpose are available at discount chains and home supply stores at a price of $20 to $25. Sales often bring prices down to the $15 to $20 range. A pair of scissors and some tape are the only tools you will need, and directions are generally included. The Department of Energy estimates that a homeowner should save from $8 to $20 in energy costs annually, so the outlay should be repaid in a little over a year. If your water heater is located in an unheated part of your house, the savings should be even greater and the payoff sooner. In fact, this project provides one of the quickest payoffs available on any type of energy-saving expenditure. You may be able to find some scrap insulation batting at a construction project that a contractor has thrown away. Since this batting is essentially the same as that found in a kit, you will reduce your cost to nearly zero (you still need the tape) by keeping a sharp lookout for some discarded insulation. During installation, you must be careful not to block any doors, vents, or relief valves, especially if you have an oil or gas water heater.

80. Install a Timer on Your Water Heater

The major cost of operating a water heater is in heating the water you consume—the water for your dishwasher, washing machine, bathtub, and sink. However, the water heater also runs to heat water you do not consume. Hot water will be left in the pipes and wasted every time you turn a hot water tap on and off, for example. Your water heater must then operate to heat an equal amount of cold water which will be drawn into the tank to replace the hot water which was used. A water heater must also occasionally run just to keep the water heated to the desired temperature even though no hot water is used. In this case, energy is consumed to reheat water that is cooled as heat escapes from the water tank.

A timer on your water heater will help to reduce the energy consumed in each of the three situations mentioned. First of all, exactly what does a timer do? It simply shuts off the flow of electricity to your water heater during time periods that you select. No matter how much hot water is consumed or how much heat is lost to the outside air during that time, no electricity will be used to heat water in the tank. If you try to draw a lot of hot water during the time the unit is switched off, the water will eventually turn cold when the tank's hot water supply is used up.

How can the timer save you money? For one thing it can prevent the tank from continually heating water when you might not need hot water for a period of time—between 11:00 P.M. and 6:00 A.M., for example. In addition, if the timer has the water heater shut off when you take your evening shower or bath, cooler water will be left in the pipes and tank so that there will be less heat wasted through losses to the outside air. The installation of a timer will force you to be more careful about the amount of hot water you consume. Since the water will start to turn cooler as cold water flows into the tank to replace the hot water that is used, you may find that your showers are shorter in duration.

Timers cost about $20 on sale and are relatively easy to install, as they fit in the electric line between the heater and plug (don't forget to turn off the breaker switch first). You will need wire cutters, a screwdriver, and a pair of pliers. The unit will allow you to turn the heating unit off and on three or four times per 24 hours. Your decision on how to adjust the timing depends upon your lifestyle and you may need to experiment. One suggestion is to have the timer shut off the water heater before you take your nightly bath. You can then set it to turn on before you rise in the morning. If your family is gone during the day you might also have the timer set to turn the heater on for only a short period in the early morning (from 5:00 to 6:00 A.M., for example). This will assure that you have hot water when you rise but the water heater will not be reheating any water as you draw it from the tank (i.e., cooler water will be left in the pipes and tank to reduce losses). A timer is probably more appropriate for a small family, and it can be used only on an electric water heater.

81. Install a Flow Restrictor on Your Shower

A cheap, easy, and good method for reducing the amount of water you consume while showering is to install a flow restrictor in the pipe at the shower head. These inexpensive devices (about $3) are easy to install and can result in considerable savings. Installation merely requires that you unscrew the shower head from the threaded pipe, insert the hinged end of the flow restrictor into the shower head, and then screw the shower head back onto the pipe and tighten with an adjustable wrench.

The idea of a restrictor is to reduce the amount of water flowing out of the shower head while at the same time producing a spray that is sufficiently strong for washing. The principle is the same as when you place your thumb over the end of a hose in order to get the water spray to go a greater distance by increasing the pressure. A restrictor can reduce the flow of water from a normal 8 gallons of water per minute to a flow of only 3 or 4 gallons and still provide a spray that is adequate for washing. Restrictors with various flow rates are available in most plumbing supply houses.

The Department of Energy estimates that the installation of this device should save the average family about $24 per year. Not a bad return for a $3 investment and a few minutes of time. Of course, actual savings depend upon how many showers are taken (the more showers the more the savings), how long family members keep the water running (more savings result from longer showers), and the temperature of the water used (the higher the temperature the greater the savings). Savings also depend upon how your water is heated, since the reduced need for heating water is the main reason for the savings. Thus, savings would be less if a gas water heater rather than an electric water heater is used.

82. Wash Your Clothes in Warm or Cold Water

Did you know that the biggest energy use in washing clothes consists of heating the water that is consumed? The electricity required to actually run the machine is small potatoes compared to what it takes to heat the water. Thus, it is possible to save a considerable amount on your electric or gas bill by reducing the amount of hot water that is consumed by your washing machine.

Although water consumption among washing machines varies by brand and model, a typical unit uses a total of about 35 gallons of water to complete the full wash and rinse cycles. The portion of hot water included in this 35 gallons depends upon which washing sequence you use. Estimates for the various cycles are as follows (KWH = kilowatt-hours—see number 78):

Cycle	Hot Water Consumed	Electricity to Heat Water
Hot wash, warm rinse	31 gallons	7.8 KWH
Hot wash, cold rinse	25 gallons	6.3 KWH
Warm wash, warm rinse	22 gallons	5.5 KWH
Warm wash, cold rinse	11 gallons	2.8 KWH
Cold wash, cold rinse	0 gallons	0.0 KWH

Considering that electricity consumed in the actual operation of a washing machine (excluding heating of water) is only about one-third kilowatt-hour, it is clear that the major cost of washing clothes is in heating wash and rinse water. And how much money can you save by being careful of the setting you use on your washing machine? Assuming you wash a load of clothes per day and that electricity costs 5 cents per kilowatt-hour where you live, the cost of heating water for washing will be:

Cycle	Cost per Load	Monthly Cost	Annual Cost
Hot wash, warm rinse	39.0¢	$11.70	$140.40
Hot wash, cold rinse	31.5	9.45	113.40
Warm wash, warm rinse	27.5	8.25	99.00
Warm wash, cold rinse	14.0	4.20	50.40
Cold wash, cold rinse	0	0	0

Thus, substituting the warm-wash, cold-rinse cycle for the hot-wash, warm-rinse cycle every time you wash a load of clothes should save about $90 annually if you average a load of clothes per day. If your washing requirements are heavier or if electricity costs over 5 cents per kilowatt-hour where you live, then the savings will be greater. On the other hand, if you wash less frequently, heat water by gas rather than electricity, or have your water heater turned to a low temperature setting, the savings will be less.

For increased savings you should use the cold-water wash where possible. In most cases it is doubtful that you will be able to detect the difference in the results, and your clothing should last longer as a result of using cold water.

83. If Your Home Has an Oil Furnace, Install a Smaller Nozzle on the Burner

Believe it or not, most oil-heated homes have heating units that are too large to be efficient. A correct-sized system should have to run almost continuously on the coldest days of the year. A study by the Department of Energy found that most homes using oil heat have heating systems so large that they run less than 30% of the time, even on the coldest days.

A heating system that is too large actually burns more oil per hour even though it is idle much of the time. In addition, during these periods when the heater is not in operation, greater drafts of hot air are lost up the flue.

If your system is oversized (and the odds are that it is), one of the least expensive methods of lowering your heating oil bill is to have your service technician install a smaller nozzle in the burner the next time he makes a service call. The technician should be able to determine the approximate nozzle size that would be most efficient for your house and climate. If he is unfamiliar with the tests, however, a list of technical instructions is available from the Department of Energy (see address below).

Assuming your unit is too large, how much will a smaller nozzle cost and what can it be expected to save? A new nozzle should cost only about $5 or $6. Adding to this the fee for a service call and a charge for filing and resetting the points which carry an electric arc to ignite the oil spray, the total cost should run from $40 to $50. Of course, if you are having your unit serviced anyway, the cost of the service call should not be included in the comparison. The Department of Energy estimates that a proper-sized nozzle should produce oil savings of from 4 to 8%. If your average annual heating bill runs about $1,000, you should be able to pay the entire cost of nozzle installation with first-year savings.

For more information on this write Technical Information Center, Department of Energy, P.O. Box 62, Oak Ridge, Tennessee 37830, and ask for *How to Improve the Efficiency of Your Oil-Fired Furnace*. It's free.

84. Don't Use Your Fireplace When It Is Really Cold Outside

A fireplace (as distinguished from a wood stove or furnace) is not particularly good at heating a home. In fact, the typical fireplace is at its very worst during the periods you would most like to use it—when the outside temperature is quite low.

Most fireplaces provide only radiant heat, with the vast majority of energy released from the burning wood being wasted up the chimney. Studies show that a typical masonry fireplace utilizes only 5 to 10% of the available heat. Unfortunately, this is only part of the problem, since fireplaces must draw air from the rest of the house in order to burn. As this air is consumed in the combustion process, it must be replaced by unheated outside air which seeps in under doors or through cracks in the house. A typical fire consumes approximately 500 to 600 cubic feet of air per minute, so that the air in a 1,400-square-foot house will have to be replaced and heated every 20 minutes.

Once you understand how the fireplace works, it is relatively easy to see that the colder the outside air, the more likely a nice cozy fire is to be an energy loser. In fact, once the outside temperature drops below freezing, there is a good chance that a burning fireplace will result in a net heat loss. Think of the energy it takes to raise an entire houseful of air from 20 to 65°F every 20 minutes. Additional heat will be lost as the fire slowly dies since the damper cannot be closed until embers are completely out. A fireplace is probably most effective when the outdoor temperature is somewhere between 40 and 50°F.

Although a fireplace may be a loser when it comes to heating a home, there are some actions you can take to reduce the amount of heat loss.

1. Close off the room where the fireplace is located when you have a fire.

2. Install tight-fitting glass doors and close them when your fire is dying out.

3. Once the fire is burning, reduce the damper opening so the fire will burn more slowly.

4. Keep a large log at the back of the fire to increase the amount of heat that is radiated.

5. Do not build a fire when the outside temperature is too low.

If you are interested in more information on fireplaces, wood stoves, or cleaning your chimney, try your local Department of Agriculture extension service. The popularity of this subject area has resulted in some excellent publications (mostly free) from this source.

85. Don't Get Burned Buying Firewood

With an increasing number of families using wood stoves, prefabricated fireplaces, and wood furnaces to try to offset the rising cost of heating their homes from ordinary sources, it is becoming more important to make sure that wood buying is done with open eyes. This is of particular concern since the increased demand for wood has resulted in higher firewood prices.

The basic measure of wood volume is the standard or full cord—a pile 8 feet wide and 4 feet high with sticks cut 4 feet in length. Because most firewood is not cut in 4-foot lengths, a more common measure, called the face cord, has come into use. This is the same size pile as the full cord except that the stick lengths are less than 4 feet. Typical lengths are 12, 16, or 24 inches. Since a face cord contains significantly less wood volume than a full cord, the cost should also be less. When firewood is sold by the truckload, the amount of wood you get is determined by the size of the truck's bed. A half-ton truck can be expected to deliver about a third of a full cord. If you are paying by the cord, measure the stack before the seller leaves in order to make sure you are getting what you are paying for.

To get the most for your money, it is best to buy hardwoods, which burn longer and produce better coals. Although hardwood is generally somewhat more difficult to light, it contains most heat value per volume (but not per pound) than do softwoods such as pine, elm, and poplar. Among the best in terms of heat value are oak, hickory, and locust. When ordering wood ask what species is being advertised and then make sure it is the type that is delivered. You should pay a lower price for the same volume of a less desirable species.

Dry wood is more desirable than wet or green wood for three reasons. First, green wood deposits more creosote in chimneys which may eventually result in a chimney fire. Second, wet wood produces less usable heat because energy is wasted in evaporating moisture before the wood will burn. As a result, green wood contains about 15% less heating value than wood of the same species that has been seasoned six months. A third reason to prefer dry wood is that you may end up getting more wood for your money. This will be the case if you buy wood by the truckload, since the drier the wood, the more a truck can carry. Ask the dealer whether wet or seasoned wood is being advertised. If both are available, specify the dry variety. If only wet wood is available, you should order in the spring. Not only will this give the wood sufficient time to season, but you may be able to obtain a better price.

For additional information on this subject, an excellent 20-page free publication, *Heating with Wood,* is available by writing Department of Energy, Technical Information Center, P.O. Box 62, Oak Ridge, Tennessee 37830.

chapter eleven

Stretching transportation dollars

86. If You Buy a Car, Make It a Small One

Remember when you drove that big clunker covered with about 50 pounds of chrome into the gas station and filled it up with 26 gallons of premium at 26 cents per gallon? Seems like a hundred years ago, doesn't it? The chrome is now replaced by plastic, the 26-gallon gas tanks are no more, premium gas is difficult to locate, and gasoline cannot be found for 26 cents a quart, let alone 26 cents a gallon.

All of these changes have been accompanied by a disappearance of large cars—and for good reason. Big cars generally cost more to buy, cost more to operate, and retain less of their value at resale. From a strictly economic viewpoint a person should own a small car. This does not mean that anyone with a large car should rush out and trade it for a small model. If you currently own a big car, you have already absorbed a large portion of the high cost as a result of the high price you paid (if you bought it new) and the relatively low resale value it now has. Unless you drive the car a lot of miles every year, the economics of trading it for a new small car are probably against you. However, if you have made a decision to purchase another automobile, be it new or used, you will save money by limiting your selection to as small a model as you can live with.

Small cars are less expensive to own in nearly every cost category. The biggest savings are due to the lower depreciation a small-car owner suffers. Even though new compact and subcompact cars are starting to cost nearly as much as their bigger counterparts, they generally bring a better price at the time of resale, so the loss in value is less. If you are a person that likes to buy a new car, keep it two or three years, and then trade in for another new one, the lower depreciation cost of owning a compact or subcompact car as opposed to a standard-size model is quite large. On the other hand, if you typically purchase a new car and keep it until it falls apart, the savings in depreciation will be less important.

In addition to lower depreciation expense, small cars use less gasoline, produce less tire wear, may involve lower-cost maintenance, and are usually less expensive to insure. When all these items are added to the lower depreciation, the savings from owning a small car are significant. A 1980 report by the Department of Transportation estimated that it cost approximately 33% less to buy and own a 1979 subcompact than a standard model of the same year. This average cost difference was based upon buying the car new, keeping it for 10 years, and driving it a total of 100,000 miles. Overall, the cost per mile for four different classes of vehicles was found to be: passenger van, 36.2 cents; standard, 24.6 cents; compact, 21.7 cents; and subcompact, 18.5 cents. While the costs are higher now, the differences in cost between each type are still relevant. For a free copy of *Cost of Owning and Operating Automobiles and Vans, 1979,* write Federal Highway Administration, Department of Transportation, Washington, D.C. 20590. The booklet also includes a worksheet showing how to calculate the cost of owning your own car.

87. Don't Be Afraid to Spend Money to Repair an Older Car

So you just received a $200 repair estimate on your sick car and have just about decided to trade in the clunker for a new model. After all, as the old saying goes, "Spending cash to repair an old car is wasted because you will never recover the money." As with most other generalizations, this one is only partially true. It is correct that you may be unable to recover the costs of certain repairs when you sell or trade your car. However, if you are spending money to keep a car running so that you do not have to buy a newer model, it is a whole different ballgame.

Two major costs of driving are minimized by driving an older car—

depreciation and the income that is lost on the money you have tied up in a car. Since newer cars nearly always lose more value every year than do their older counterparts, keeping your old car will help to beat this trap. In fact, after nine or ten years an automobile generally stops losing value because it has little resale value remaining. The reduction in depreciation expense in keeping your old car is a relatively easy concept to grasp.

The idea of lost income is more difficult to visualize, especially if you pay cash for a car. Suppose your old car would bring about $1,000 if you were to sell it. If you feel you could invest this money to provide a 10% return, then you are losing $100 (10% of $1,000) per year by having funds invested in the car rather than in the alternative investment. However, if you were to sell your car and purchase a newer model for $7,000, you would have to invest an additional $6,000. Assuming you are paying cash to cover the difference, you will be foregoing an annual income of $700 rather than $100 with the old car. Thus, trading cars results in an additional cost of $600 annually, even if you pay cash. If you borrow the money for the new purchase, the cost will be even greater. Of course, you must adjust this lost income for any additional income taxes you would have to pay. By the time you consider both the loss of investment income and the extra depreciation, however, it should be clear that a person can afford to spend a lot of money repairing an old car in order to keep from trading in on a newer model.

You must also consider that newer cars result in higher insurance bills and will mean additional property taxes in many states. And except in the few states that have no sales tax, you will have to pay a significant amount of sales tax every time you trade in cars. If you have new car fever, take two aspirin, drink a lot of liquids, and consider how much money you are saving with your old clunker.

88. Change Your Automobile Oil and Oil Filter Yourself

One of the most frequent maintenance jobs on a car is the changing of motor oil and oil filter. Fortunately, this is also one of the easiest (but not necessarily the cleanest) chores that can be performed by the car owner. Although some individuals only replace filters during every other oil change, many mechanics suggest changing the filter every time. When you perform the job yourself you might as well change the filter also since the additional cost is so small.

If you have no mechanical ability, where do you get started? First, look through the owner's manual of your car, as it will probably provide directions. Next, find the locations of the oil filter and oil drain plug. If you are still unsure whether you can accomplish the job yourself, take the car to a service station that is offering a special on the service (check your newspaper) and watch each step that the mechanic takes. If you don't understand something he is doing, ask him about it. Following this you should be able to do the job the next time by yourself.

To get started you will need to buy an oil drain pan (something to drain the old oil into), a filter wrench (to get the old oil filter off your car), and a funnel or nozzle (to pour fresh oil into the car). These can be obtained as an oil change kit at most discount stores (K Mart or Woolco). You will also need a wrench to loosen the drain plug. Check your owner's manual to see what size filter is required (the store should know) and what type of oil is recommended (you can't go wrong with 10W40 weight). Now shop around and look for sales. Believe it or not, you may well be able to buy these on special for a lower price than a service station pays. You should be able to buy a filter for under $2 and good oil for less than $1 per quart. If you find an especially good price, buy two or three filters and a case of oil.

How much can you save? If your car uses four quarts of oil, this would result in a cost of $3.60 (4 $\times$ 95 cents per quart) plus $1.80 for the filter, or $5.40 total. A station will charge you two or three times this amount.

One last word. Don't forget to wear old clothes and to spread newspapers under the car. Also remember that your car will need an occasional lube job. The owner's manual will tell you how often you need to take the car to a service station for this inexpensive service.

89. Pay Cash for Gasoline

Even though gasoline is not in the abundant supply it once was, it is still possible for a driver to save money by price shopping for this product. In fact, it may be possible to save 20 cents or more per gallon by spending a little time and effort to compare prices at a number of stations. Often it is the small independent operators that offer the lowest prices.

One of the greatest deterrents to gasoline price shopping is the use of an oil company credit card. By using one of these, you will find yourself spending time looking for a particular brand of gasoline instead of a station that offers the lowest prices. Of course, the oil companies know this, which is why they issue their own credit cards in the first place. Although some stations will accept credit cards issued by nearly any major oil company, you cannot always count on it. In fact, some stations that offer the lowest prices sell only for cash (national credit card companies such as Visa and MasterCard levy a fee on stations when customers use their cards).

Many individuals have found oil company credit cards particularly useful during vacation trips when it is necessary to drive many miles and purchase a lot of gasoline. After all, it is more convenient to be able to pull out some plastic than to have to carry a lot of cash that might be lost or stolen. However, even here it may be to your advantage to pay for gasoline purchases by means of traveler's checks rather than credit cards. Traveler's checks provide you with the flexibility to choose stations offering the lowest prices while at the same time overcoming the disadvantage of possible loss, since lost traveler's checks are generally easily replaced.

Even if you do not have access to no-fee traveler's checks (ask your credit union or bank, since you may be eligible to purchase these at no fee and not realize it), the normal fee of 1% of the face amount of checks purchased will be easily outweighed by the savings from lower gasoline prices.

90. Check the Quality Rating When Buying New Tires

You notice that the two back tires on your automobile are getting badly worn and know you must soon purchase new ones. Being a conscientious shopper, you decide to scour the Sunday newspaper and look for the best price. The pages are loaded with tire advertisements and every dealer in town seems to be having a sale. The cheapest tires in your size appear to be at Auto World, where the price is two for $60. On the facing page, Tire Heaven is selling the same-size tires for $35 each. One of the large retail chains is running a special on that size at two for $65, and a discount store is having a sale at four for $125. Are the least expensive tires the best buy, or is there really any way to know?

Until recently, it was essentially impossible for consumers to make informed decisions when buying tires because there was no uniform method of grading tire quality. Manufacturers would assign names such as "economy," "premium," and "first-quality" to their products in such a way that the words were virtually meaningless to the public. The economy tire might actually be the most expensive line because of the poor mileage it delivers. Likewise, one manufacturer's premium grade might be no better than another producer's second-line brand.

Take heart. In 1979, the Department of Transportation instituted the Uniform Tire Quality Grading System that rates three important performance characteristics of passenger tires: treadwear, traction, and temperature resistance. The grades of each characteristic are molded onto the side of every tire.

Treadwear is shown as an index with 100 representing average. Other index numbers then signify the mileage you should expect from a particular tire with respect to one that is average. For example, a tire with a treadwear grade of 130 should provide 30% more miles than a tire with a grade of 100 (assuming you properly care for the tires). An index, rather than expected mileage, is used because wear on a given tire is affected by road conditions and driving habits. Thus, there is no reason to expect that the same tire will produce equal mileage for a 25-year-old driver in Texas and a 60-year-old driver in Oregon. There is reason to believe that, for the same driver, a tire with a grade of 90 will produce only 90% of the miles of a tire with a grade of 100.

Traction is determined by a tire's ability to stop a car on wet roads. Grading runs from A to C, with A representing superior traction and C indicating poor traction.

Since high sustained temperatures can lead to deterioration of a tire's materials and result in a blowout or tread separation, resistance to heat buildup can be very important. Temperature resistance is graded on the basis of A, B, and C ratings, with A representing a tire with a superior ability to "run cool."

Now that you know there is a grading system, how can you use it? First decide how important traction and temperature resistance are for your type of driving. If you do a lot of high-speed highway driving, for example, you may need a tire with a grade A for temperature resistance. On the other hand, if the tires are for a car used for town driving, you may find grades B or C to be acceptable. Once you have determined the traction and temperature resistance ratings you need, use the treadwear grade to determine the best buy while keeping in mind how long you plan to keep the car.

For a free brochure on tire quality grading write National Highway

Traffic Safety Administration, Department of Transportation, Washington, D.C. 20590. The department also has ratings for individual brands, but you will have to pay for this (5 cents per page or about $7 for a complete list).

91. Buy a Tire Air Pressure Gauge

"Want your tires checked?" This is a voice out of the past whose absence is almost surely costing you money. The reason is that all tires slowly lose air, and automobiles driven on underinflated tires get reduced gasoline mileage. And because more drivers are pumping their own gasoline at self-service stations and the attendants at full-service stations are generally skipping this maintenance, a greater number of cars are being driven on underinflated tires. In fact, one study found that 28% of the tires it tested were severely underinflated. Even if you remember to have your tires checked when you buy gasoline, you have a problem—pressure should be checked when the tires are cold (i.e., when they have been sitting for three hours or before driving one mile) since recommended pressures are nearly always for cold tires. Warm tires produce higher pressure readings.

A simple answer to this problem is to buy your own pressure gauge. It will not be very expensive (about $2) and is easily found in the automotive department of nearly any discount store. The advantage of having your own gauge is that it makes it possible to check your tire pressure at home when your tires are cool so that you will know how much air to add when you reach a service station.

When you add air pressure, use close to the maximum recommended pressure marked on the tire rather than that which is in the owner's manual. Many manuals recommend a lower pressure that will result in a smoother ride (but lower mileage). However, you should maintain any recommended pressure difference between front and back tires.

So how much can you save by making this $2 investment? A report to the Department of Transportation estimated that every 2 pounds of additional pressure in bias-ply tires improves gas mileage by 1 to 1½%. Thus, proper pressure in tires that are normally underinflated by 4 to 6 pounds should result in increased mileage of 5 to 6%. With a car that gets 20 miles per gallon and is driven 12,000 miles per year this means a savings of approximately 30 gallons of gasoline annually. If you have radial tires or drive mostly in town, the savings will be somewhat less.

92. Think Twice about Buying a Recreational Vehicle

How many times have you seen pictures of Colorado's mountains or Yellowstone National Park's geysers and wished you were there? If you are thinking of seeing those sites from the seat of a new recreational vehicle, you had best sit back and decide if that is really the way to go. Recreational vehicles are expensive to buy, cost a lot to operate and insure, and are generally difficult to store when not in use. Perhaps there is a better way to accomplish your goal.

Owning a recreational vehicle (RV) entails a number of costs and headaches that first-time buyers may overlook. For the most part, individuals accept the relatively poor gas mileage, which may well run under 10 miles per gallon. If you are planning a 6,000-mile trip in a RV that gets 10 miles to the gallon, your gasoline bill will run about $720 (600 gallons @ $1.20 per gallon). This is $430 more than the same trip would cost in a car that obtains 25 miles per gallon. You will also find higher costs for tires, oil changes, and other maintenance items than you would for an automobile. In fact, you may actually find it difficult to get a big RV serviced on the road.

Another major expense of owning a recreational vehicle is related to the money you must invest. Suppose you purchase a moderately priced RV for $20,000 (they run much higher). Even when you pay cash you will forego $2,000 in yearly income you could otherwise have earned on the funds (assuming a return of 10%). If you are lucky and have a four-week vacation coming up, you are talking about a $500 per week cost from the lost income alone. And what about depreciation? When you decide to sell the vehicle the price you receive will depend upon a number of factors, including availability of gasoline and prices of new RVs. Suppose we hope for the best and assume your vehicle loses value at a rate of only $1,000 per year. If you use it four weeks a year, you are actually talking about depreciation of $250 per week. You will also have extra insurance, more taxes, and a new license plate to buy. And you may find that it is too unsightly or even illegal to park a big recreational vehicle at your home and thus necessary to pay a monthly fee to store it across town.

So what is the extra cost of that four-week trip to the Rockies?

Gasoline (@10 mpg)	$ 720
Opportunity cost of money in RV	2,000

Depreciation	1,000
Maintenance (@6¢ per mile)	360
Insurance, taxes, and tag	500
Camping fees (@$6 per night)	168
Total	$4,748

or about $1,200 per week. If you are able to utilize the RV for a lesser amount of time the cost will be proportionately higher on a weekly basis. If you think this overstates the cost of owning a recreational vehicle, just buy one and see how fast the money seeps from your pocket. In fact, you will be lucky if you get off this cheaply.

It is possible to control part of this huge cost. One of the major disadvantages of most recreational vehicles is that they are not useful for ordinary driving. If you can get by with a small van and can also use it as your source of everyday transportation, the costs of a camping vacation can be cut way back, since you would have many of the expenses anyway. For example, you would have no additional costs for depreciation, opportunity cost, insurance, taxes, and tag because you use the vehicle for camping. You might also consider renting a RV unit. This may be a wise move if this is to be your maiden voyage on the camping scene. Of course, there is always the least expensive way to go—tenting.

93. Shop around for an Airline Ticket

You probably think that if you are flying from Jacksonville, Florida to Denver via Atlanta (a purgatory for air travelers in the Southeast) on Tuesday at 10:00 A.M. and returning on the following Sunday at 2:00 P.M., there is a single ticket price that applies to your journey. Well, you may be right, but it is doubtful that anyone knows exactly what that price should be. Airline rates have become so complicated that even the majority of airline personnel do not seem to fathom them. And if they do understand them, it is unlikely that they know all the options available. There are joint fares, excursion fares, day fares, special saver fares, night fares and, presumably, even regular fares.

To give you an example of the impossible maze of airline ticket prices, let me cite my own recent experience. In checking on a roundtrip fare from Valdosta, Georgia to Monroe, Louisiana (via Atlanta, of course),

I was told that the least expensive ticket involved a joint fare with another airline and would cost $334. I ordered the ticket and told them I would pick it up at the airport on the morning of the flight. When I arrived at the airport I found to my dismay that the clerk had written the ticket at a price of $380 because, he said, my layover in the Atlanta airport was too long to qualify for a joint fare. During the Atlanta layover, I complained to the ticket agent and found that the joint fare was okay (I was scheduled on the first available plane) but that the $380 charge was actually too low for regular fare anyway (it should have been slightly over $400). When I returned home I was to learn that I actually qualified for the excursion rate of $264. Four different opinions resulted in four different fare possibilities.

The chance of receiving different fare quotes on the same ticket is more likely the more complicated your trip. If you are routed through two or more airports, are required to fly on at least two carriers, and will be gone long enough to qualify for an excursion rate, the possibilities are endless. If other members of your family will be traveling with you and the tickets are ordered far enough ahead to permit some of the special fares, so much the better, for the level of complexity will increase geometrically.

There are reasons other than confusion over fares to shop around for a good deal on an airline ticket. With the recent trend toward deregulation, a difference in fares is more likely among different airlines flying the same routes. For example, a small regional carrier will sometimes have a lower fare between two cities than a large national carrier. It may be that the larger line feels the small carrier is not important enough (i.e., does not carry enough passengers) to match its lower charge. Occasionally an airline will begin flying a new route and initiate special introductory fares for a few weeks. If you are able to take advantage of this fare for at least part of your trip, the savings can be significant.

So if you are accustomed to making a single call to order an airline ticket, take a little time to make a few extra inquiries. You may be able to achieve a much lower fare for your trouble.

chapter twelve

Odds and ends

94. Take Advantage of the Public Library

As the cost of recreation and leisure-time activities increases, there is one place you can go and spend no more money than you did ten years ago. The place is your local public library and the cost is still zero. The library is one of the best deals going, and yet many people still either avoid it or just plain forget about it.

If you haven't been to your library for a while, you may be in for a surprise. For one thing, many are in new buildings that are open, colorful, and well lighted. Quite a change from the dark old castles of the past. In addition, many libraries offer a variety of activities and services that were not available in times past. Films, records, storytelling or puppet shows for children, and pictures for your wall are all available at many public libraries. And it is all free.

Libraries are particularly valuable because of the rising costs of books, magazines, and newspapers. As it becomes increasingly expensive to purchase books and subscriptions to periodicals, it makes more sense to use the library. Paperback books that a few years ago cost less than a dollar now sell for between $2 and $3. At the library you can check out the hardback version for free before the paperback version even hits the stands. And rather than choosing between a subscription to *Time* or *Newsweek* or to *Sports Illustrated* or *Inside Sports* and paying a steep price whatever your choice, frequenting the library allows you to browse through all of them for free. The same goes for newspapers.

The secret to using the library is to get started. Make it a point to drop by a few times and see what it offers. You may be surprised to find that the place grows on you. Just think, substituting an evening trip to the library for going to the movies just once a month will save you $40 or $50 per year (double this if you are married or have a liberal-minded date) and you will learn more at the same time.

95. Stop Smoking (or Don't Start)

If you are a confirmed smoker you probably know it by heart: "Warning: The Surgeon General Has Determined That Cigarette Smoking Is Dangerous to Your Health." It is on the side of every pack of cigarettes you pick up. In spite of this warning and the well-known dangers, millions of people continue to puff the weed. Maybe it would help if the opposite side of the pack carried a different message: "Warning: The Secretary of the Treasury Has Determined That Cigarette Smoking Is Dangerous to Your Bank Account." Or perhaps "The Tax Commissioners Express Their Gratitude for Your Contribution."

Cigarette smoking is an expensive habit—perhaps more expensive than you realize. And the expense continues to grow as state legislatures impose higher taxes and cigarette companies raise the price of their product. Concerning oneself about the cost of smoking is difficult unless a long-term view is taken. Do not think of the cost of smoking in terms of the price of a pack of cigarettes, but rather as the expense of lots of packs of cigarettes and the things you must give up because you are a smoker.

If you are a moderate smoker, you may well consume about a carton of cigarettes per week counting those you smoke, lose, ruin, or have bummed away. Depending upon where you live, you can expect to pay anywhere from $4.00 per carton in the tobacco-growing states of Kentucky and North Carolina to $7.00 or $8.00 per carton in high-tax states like New York and Florida. If you pay somewhere between these extremes—say $6.00 a carton—you are shelling out about $300 per year. Over a ten-year period this amounts to $3,000, and not a dime of it is tax-deductible. Just think of what you could do with these savings. You could take two or three nice two-day vacations each year and not feel guilty about spending the money. You could take your spouse or date on a nice evening out once a month.

Now look at the same money from a different perspective. If you were to stop smoking and use the savings to make annual deposits of $300 into an account paying a return of 9%, you would accumulate $4,725 in ten years, $15,348 in twenty years, and $40,893 in thirty years.

The numbers may look big, but they are not unrealistic. Smoking is an expensive habit that steals your money as well as your health. So the next time you are filling out your income tax forms and start cussing the government bureaucrats, just remember the one tax that you can really do something about.

There is a way to use simple economics to make the habit even more expensive (and, hopefully, make quitting more likely). If your husband or wife smokes, ask that you be allowed an equal amount of funds as your spouse spends on cigarettes to use as you see fit. This will bring home the cost of smoking very quickly.

96. Complain about an Unsatisfactory Product or Service

Many individuals who feel they have received an unsatisfactory product or service never take their complaint any farther than their friends. They may not report their dissatisfaction back to where the product was purchased because they are too busy, because they don't feel such an action will accomplish anything, or simply because they are self-conscious about stirring up trouble. As a result, many consumer problems never get back to the place where they do the most good—both in terms of satisfying the consumer and preventing a recurrence of the problem.

As surprising as it may seem, a majority of businesses actually prefer that you register a complaint. From their point of view the very worst thing you can do is decide to avoid their product or service in the future and then tell your friends, who might also avoid it. Many companies solicit consumer comments, and one company even goes so far as to indicate an 800 toll-free telephone number on some of its products. To get yourself in the right frame of mind, consider that you are actually doing the business a favor by calling a problem to its attention.

And how should you go about registering a complaint? The place to begin the process is where you purchased the product or service. And do not bother with a sales or public relations person. Get as close to the top as early as possible. The chances are that seeing a lower-level employee will result in unnecessary delay and that the manager will eventually become involved anyway. If this doesn't work, write directly to the manufacturer or head office. The local store may provide you with a name and address, or a library or stock brokerage firm may be able to help. When writing the manufacturer be sure to include all the information relevant to your case, including what is wrong, previous complaints, place where purchased, dates, etc.

If you are still not satisfied, consider two other avenues: small claims court (discussed in the next section) and complaining to a state or federal agency. The *Consumers Resource Handbook* is an excellent source for finding out exactly where you should direct your complaints. It is available free by writing the Consumer Information Center, Dept. 532 G, Pueblo, Colorado 81009.

97. Use a Small Claims Court If You Get Ripped Off

Suppose you have just moved from an apartment and the landlord refuses to return your deposit. Or maybe the paint on your car is peeling two weeks after you paid the shop to repaint it and the owner will not return your money or repair the defect. Perhaps a mechanic put the wrong part in your car and caused considerable damage but the garage will not assume responsibility. If your claim is relatively large, you should probably seek the services of an attorney. If your claim is small, however, the best remedy may be to take your problem to small claims court.

Small claims courts are set up to handle disagreements involving small amounts of money. They allow an individual to receive a speedy and inexpensive day in court without being required to be represented by an attorney. Even though attorneys are not required, however, most states allow them to appear. As a rule, the only expense in bringing your case to the court is a small one-time filing fee, which usually varies between $3 and $8. Each state imposes a maximum amount for which you can sue. This ranges from $300 to $3,000 (it has been increasing in recent years), but generally averages about $500. If you feel you are entitled to recover an amount greater than the allowed limit, but are willing to reduce your claim to within the maximum, you may still use the court.

The atmosphere at most small claims courts is quite informal, with procedures determined, in large part, by the individual preferences of the presiding judges. Basically, the judge allows each party to state his or her side of the story before issuing a ruling. If the ruling is in your favor, you will recover all or part of the amount of your suit plus the cost of filing the claim.

To get started on your case, call the small claims court in your town or county (it is usually located in the courthouse) and ask about the filing procedure. You might also find the hours the court is open and ask the clerk if your type of case is permitted. Next you should go to the court in order to file your claim and pay the filing fee. The clerk will then set a court date and prepare to send a summons to the defendant. Prior to the hearing date you should accumulate all of the evidence (e.g., bills, contracts, canceled checks, pictures, etc.) relating to your case and talk to any witnesses you wish to appear. You may also find it quite useful to visit the court as an observer at least once before your case is heard so that you will know better what to expect on your day in court. For a free Department of Justice guide on using small claims court write: Consumer Information Center, Pueblo, Colorado 81009 and ask for *Consumers Tell It to the Judge.*

98. Send Postcards at Christmas

Believe it or not, it has not been that long ago when a person could mail a first-class letter for 8 cents. Even the 4-cent first-class stamp is still visible in the not-too-distant past. With the current cost of mailing a letter being 20 cents, this means postage costs are near the top of the list when it comes to identifying goods and services that have undergone major price increases. A painless way to partially offset the higher cost of postage is to utilize postcards. And one of the best times to substitute postcards for first-class mail is during the annual period when you probably make maximum use of the mail—Christmas. Christmastime presents a unique opportunity to save money by using postcards. Not only do most individuals mail a lot of cards during a short period, but they generally write a fairly standard message that requires only a minimum of privacy. This does not mean you have to go so far as to send plain postcards at Christmas. Rather, you should consider using some of the attractive varieties printed by the major card companies.

The use of Christmas postcards in place of regular Christmas cards has an added advantage—the former cost less to purchase even though they are often equally attractive. Postcards use less paper and do not require envelopes and so are less expensive to manufacture. These lower expenses are usually passed on to consumers in lower retail prices. Since most recipients of Christmas cards are interested only in the front design and any personal message you include, a Christmas postcard contains the essential ingredients most people appreciate.

The amount you save by substituting postcards for regular cards depends upon how many individuals are on your mailing list. The savings per card will amount to 7 cents for postage (20 cents for first-class vs. 13 cents for a postcard) plus at least 5-cents difference in the cost of the card. If you normally send 50 cards, the annual savings will equal $6.00 (12 cents per card X 50 cards).

A bonus of using postcards is that you do not feel that you have to write as long a personal message since there is not as much space available as on regular cards. Remember to buy the cards one year early so you can obtain them during the half-price sales that occur just after Christmas.

99. Make a Will

While a will won't save money during your lifetime, it may well save a significant amount of money for your spouse and children. If you die without a will (termed dying *intestate*), your estate will be distributed based upon the law in the state in which you live. In other words, if you do not have a will, the state of your residence will impose one on your estate. It is the state that will decide how your assets will be distributed.

Why do the majority of people die without leaving a will? Many individuals do not like to face the fact that they are mortal and must eventually die. Others try to avoid attorneys as much as possible. Still others do not want to have to decide how their assets should be distributed even though by not having a will they are indirectly making this decision by letting the state do the job. And many people decide that since they do not have much to leave, it really does not make much difference whether they have a will or not.

Unfortunately, dying intestate may not only result in a distribution of your assets in a way you would not approve, it may also result in the payment of more taxes than would otherwise be necessary. The federal government levies an estate tax which is calculated on the basis of the size and distribution of an estate. Likewise, state governments levy taxes that are often based upon the relationship of the deceased and the heirs. A will allows an individual to try to reduce these taxes by specifying how an estate's assets will be divided.

Another advantage of a will is that it allows a person to designate an individual to administer his or her estate according to the instructions of the will. This person, called an *executor*, will make sure that all the terms of the will are actually carried out. If no will is left, the court must appoint an executor. A will may also be used to designate a guardian for minors. If no one is designated or no will is left, a court must also make this appointment.

Hence, there are a number of good reasons to make a will. Nearly all experts in the field warn against trying to save money by purchasing a kit or writing your own will. Laws vary from state to state, and the rules are so complicated and the technicalities so great (how many people must witness your signature, for example) that employing a competent attorney is worth the money. In seeking a lawyer, shop around and look for advertisements in the newspapers. Attorneys will sometimes make wills at a very low price in order to generate other legal business. Keep in mind that it may be necessary to occasionally alter or even make out a new will as your life changes (e.g., new children, remarriage, a move to a different state).

100. Join a Memorial Society

Individuals are usually at their most vulnerable when a loved one dies. As a result, they are relatively easy targets to take advantage of when funeral arrangements are being made. Even when the spouse or children try to plan the arrangements in a rational manner, there will be difficulty in making decisions because of some of the practices found in the industry.

There is no particular reason to suspect that funeral directors are any more dishonest than any other group of businessmen. However, they are businessmen and earn their income from selling you a service. The type of service you are sold determines the income that is generated from your business. When you walk into an automobile showroom, does the salesman immediately take you to the lowest-priced model available? Of course not, and neither should you presume that the funeral director will act differently.

In addition to a funeral director's natural business instinct to sell you a higher-quality service, there are a number of questionable practices that sometimes take place to inflate the price of a funeral. These include offering a funeral at a package price without itemizing individual costs, requiring that coffins be burned during cremations (metal coffins do not burn), misstating health requirements for cremation or embalming, and automatically including extra service (at a charge) that would not normally be requested.

The major discretionary item in most funerals is the fee paid for a casket. This may be as low as a couple of hundred dollars or as high as several thousand dollars. Caskets often involve very large price markups by funeral firms. Since similar markups generate more profits on high-priced than on low-priced caskets, funeral directors may be expected to favor using the former, and their sales presentations to prospective casket buyers will often reveal this. One method is to suggest that being buried in anything other than a high-quality (and high-priced) casket is beneath the dignity of the deceased.

So how can you keep your own relatives from being oversold on funeral arrangements when you pass away? Perhaps you should consider joining a memorial society. Memorial societies are organizations designed to help members arrange relatively simple funeral services. While the societies do not take care of the funeral arrangements themselves, they do allow a member to predetermine the type and price of the funeral service that is desired. There are currently 180 societies in the United States and an additional 25 in Canada. These organizations represent approximately a million members. There is a small one-time charge for joining a memorial society. For general information on what the societies do and how to become a member write Continental Association of Funeral and Memorial Societies, Inc., 1828 L Street N.W., Washington, D.C. 20036, and ask for their brochure *Funeral and Memorial Societies*. It is free but you will make their life easier by including a stamped, self-addressed envelope. They will also provide a pamphlet on funeral planning, but this will cost you a quarter.

101. Think about Bankruptcy If Things Really Go to Pot

Suppose you have gotten so far into debt that it is no longer possible to see any chance of getting out. You owe thousands on your house, the loans on your automobiles amount to more than the cars are actually worth, you have personal loans outstanding with the bank, credit union, and three finance companies, you owe money to four or five stores for merchandise purchased, and you are borrowed up to the limit on your credit cards. It is possible for a person to finally reach the point where the requirements for servicing debt are so great that it is impossible to make the payments from current or expected income. The hopelessness of such a situation can make that person unproductive in an economic sense.

In an effort to help these people become productive, the government allows individuals to try to make themselves whole again by declaring personal bankruptcy. Essentially, declaring personal bankruptcy allows individuals to legally wipe out their debts by giving up their assets. If you have a lot more in debts than you do in assets, you can see that this may not be so bad after all. There are some restrictions, however. First of all, you are not released from all of your debts. Alimony, child support, back taxes, educational loans, and debts for goods and services received under false pretenses are among those obligations you cannot discharge through bankruptcy. In addition, once you declare bankruptcy you must wait at least six years before doing so again.

While you cannot use bankruptcy to wash away all your debts, you are able to retain a portion of your assets. The exemptions may vary somewhat from state to state, but if you own the property outright you will probably be entitled to keep $7,500 of equity in your home, jewelry worth up to $500, unmatured life insurance, a motor vehicle worth up to $1,200, personal items worth up to $200 each, and tools of your trade worth up to $750. Also exempted are income from disability, alimony, child support payments, Social Security, and unemployment benefits. If you do not own particular property outright (e.g., it is something being used as collateral for a loan), the bankruptcy trustee will decide whether to sell the property or give it up to the creditor.

After you file for bankruptcy, the court will notify your creditors and a date will be set for a hearing before a court-appointed referee. Prior to the hearing you are required to make out a list of all your assets and liabilities. If you employ an attorney to assist you, it is a good bet you will have to pay his or her fee up front in cash.

There is a less severe type of bankruptcy called Chapter 13 (the plan just discussed is Chapter 7) or the Wage Earner Plan. Under this procedure an individual and a counselor prepare a plan to repay debts over a period of time. If both the creditors and the court agree, this plan will protect you from being hounded while you make payments to the court and, in turn, the court pays your creditors. Under this plan you are permitted to keep your assets so long as you continue making the agreed-upon payments.

While this description of bankruptcy may sound like a cure-all, it is not. All it does is get you off the hook and allow a fresh beginning. The excesses that both you and your creditors engaged in will have to be eliminated or you will soon be back in the same shape. Also be aware that this is a relatively simple treatment of a complicated topic, and you will almost surely need the help of an attorney if you actually go this route. For additional information write Administrative Office of the United States Courts, Division of Bankruptcy, Washington, D.C. 20544.

Index